Mapping Data Flows in Azure Data Factory

Building Scalable ETL Projects in the Microsoft Cloud

Mark Kromer

Apress®

Mapping Data Flows in Azure Data Factory: Building Scalable ETL Projects in the Microsoft Cloud

Mark Kromer
SNOHOMISH, WA, USA

ISBN-13 (pbk): 978-1-4842-8611-1   ISBN-13 (electronic): 978-1-4842-8612-8
https://doi.org/10.1007/978-1-4842-8612-8

Managing Director, Apress Media LLC: Welmoed Spahr
Acquisitions Editor: Jonathan Gennick
Development Editor: Laura Berendson
Coordinating Editor: Jill Balzano

Cover designed by eStudioCalamar

Cover image designed by Freepik (www.freepik.com)

Distributed to the book trade worldwide by Springer Science+Business Media New York, 1 New York Plaza, Suite 4600, New York, NY 10004-1562, USA. Phone 1-800-SPRINGER, fax (201) 348-4505, e-mail orders-ny@springer-sbm.com, or visit www.springeronline.com. Apress Media, LLC is a California LLC and the sole member (owner) is Springer Science + Business Media Finance Inc (SSBM Finance Inc). SSBM Finance Inc is a **Delaware** corporation.

For information on translations, please e-mail booktranslations@springernature.com; for reprint, paperback, or audio rights, please e-mail bookpermissions@springernature.com.

Apress titles may be purchased in bulk for academic, corporate, or promotional use. eBook versions and licenses are also available for most titles. For more information, reference our Print and eBook Bulk Sales web page at http://www.apress.com/bulk-sales.

Any source code or other supplementary material referenced by the author in this book is available to readers on GitHub (https://github.com/Apress). For more detailed information, please visit http://www.apress.com/source-code.

Printed on acid-free paper

*This book is dedicated to my loving wife Stacy and
our boys Ethan and Jude. Thank you for putting up with
my late hours working on data analytics and writing this book!*

Table of Contents

About the Author

Mark Kromer has been in the data analytics product space for over 20 years and is currently a Principal Program Manager for Microsoft's Azure data integration products. Mark often writes and speaks on big data analytics and data analytics and was an engineering architect and product manager for Oracle, Pentaho, AT&T, and Databricks prior to Microsoft Azure.

About the Technical Reviewer

 **Andy Leonard** is a husband, dad, and grandfather; creator of – and Data Philosopher at – DILM Suite for Data Integration Lifecycle Management (dilmsuite.com); a blogger (andyleonard.blog); founder and Chief Data Engineer at Enterprise Data & Analytics (entdna.com); an SSIS and Azure Data Factory trainer, consultant, and developer; a SQL Server database and data warehouse developer; and an author, mentor, engineer, and farmer.

Introduction

The ETL (extract, transform, load) process has been a cornerstone of data warehouses, data marts, and business intelligence for decades. ETL is how data engineers have traditionally refined raw data into business analytics that guide the business to make better decisions. These projects have allowed engineers to build up libraries of common ETL processes and practices from traditional on-premises data warehouses over the years, very commonly with data coming from Oracle, Microsoft, IBM, or Sybase databases or business ERP/CRM applications like Salesforce, SAP, Dynamics, etc. However, over the past decade, our industry has seen these analytical workloads migrate to the cloud at a very rapid pace.

To keep up with these changes, we've had to adjust ETL techniques to account for more varied and larger data. The big data revolution and cloud migrations have forced us to rethink many of our proven ETL patterns to meet modern data transformation challenges and demands. Today, the vast majority of data that we process exists primarily in the cloud. And that data may not always be governed and curated by rigid business processes in the way that our previous ETL processes could rely on.

The common scenarios of processing well-known hardened schemas from SAP and CSV exports will now have a new look and challenge. The data sources will likely vary in shape, size, and scope from day to day. We need to account for schema drift, data drift, and other possible obstructions to refining data in a way that turns the data into refined business analytics.

Cloud-First ETL with Mapping Data Flows

Welcome to *Mapping Data Flows in Azure Data Factory*! In this book, I'm going to introduce you to Microsoft Azure Data Factory and the Mapping Data Flows feature in ADF as the key ETL toolset to tackle these modern data analytics challenges. As you make your way through the book, you'll learn key concepts, and through the use of examples, you'll begin to build your first cloud-based ETL projects that can help you to unlock the potential of scaled-out big data ETL processing in the cloud. I'll demonstrate how to tackle the particularly difficult and challenging aspects of big data analytics and how to prepare data for business decision makers in the cloud.

To get the most value from this book, you should have a firm understanding of building data warehouses and business intelligence projects. It is not necessary to have many hours of experience building cloud-first big data analytics projects already. However, having some experience in cloud computing will provide valuable context that will help you as you work through some of these new approaches.

The examples and scenarios used in this book will be patterns and practices that are based on ETL common scenarios, so having data engineering experience and background will also be very helpful. I'll help guide you along as you migrate from traditional on-premises data engineering to the world of Azure Data Factory.

Overview of Azure Data Factory

To become familiar with the data engineering process in Microsoft Azure, we'll need to begin with an overview of Azure Data Factory (ADF), which is the Azure service for building data pipelines. The first chapter will focus on conceptual discussions of how to build a process to transform massive of amounts of data with many quality issues in the cloud. Essentially, we need to redefine ETL for cloud-based big data, where data volumes and veracity can change daily, and we'll compare and contrast the Azure mechanism for the modern data engineer with traditional ETL. That's where we'll begin the process of building ETL pipelines that will serve as the basis for your big data analytics projects. I'm going to present a series of common use cases that will demonstrate how to apply the concepts discussed in the earlier chapters to practical ETL projects. From there, the focus will turn to a deep dive on Mapping Data Flows and how to build ETL frameworks in ADF by using the visual design-time interface to build code-free data flows. Mapping Data Flows is primarily a code-free visual design experience, so we'll walk through techniques and best practices for managing the software development life cycle of a data flow in ADF. Data Factory provides many different means to process and transform data that include coding and calling external compute processes. However, in this book, the focus will be on building ETL pipelines in a code-free style in Mapping Data Flows.

As you work your way through the early chapters in this book, you should begin to develop an understanding of how to apply data engineering principles in ADF and Mapping Data Flows. That's where we'll begin to implement mechanisms to help organize your work and design-time environment, preparing for eventual operationalization at runtime. We'll set up a Git repo for our work, as you should in real-life scenarios. We'll design interactive data transformation graphs using serverless compute that can scale out as needed. You won't need to manage physical servers and clusters with ADF, but I will explain how things work behind the scenes to provide this serverless compute power for your pipelines. Behind the scenes, ADF will leverage the Azure platform-as-a-service workflow engine Logic Apps for pipeline execution and scheduling. The transformation engine for Mapping Data Flows is Apache Spark. But you won't have to learn anything about those underlying dependent services. The Azure Integration Runtimes will provide that compute for you dynamically in a serverless manner.

Operationalizing Data Pipelines

As you begin designing data flows for cloud-first big data workloads, we will test and debug in nonproduction environments and then promote that work to production environments. Execution of those jobs will be performed via ADF data pipelines based on schedules. These chapters will focus on operationalizing our work in a way that will become the eventual automated ETL framework for your business analytics. A complete end-to-end solution must also require monitoring and management of these processes on an ongoing basis. The final chapters will provide mechanisms in ADF that can be leveraged to monitor runs over time and to examine the performance of your pipelines. Because the nature of big data in the cloud is that the data will be messy and ever-changing, it is important to establish alerts and handling for schema and data drift. I'll explain how to add fail-safe mechanisms, monitoring, and traps for these common problems so that your data pipelines can execute continuously. The frameworks needed for design, debug, schedule, monitor, and manage are all contained inside of ADF, and we'll spend time digging into each one of those areas.

Goal for the Book

My goal is that by the end of this book, you'll be able to apply the concepts and the patterns presented here to build ETL pipelines for your next big data analytics project in the cloud. By mapping these new, updated approaches to processing data for analytics (a.k.a. big data analytics) to the world of traditional ETL processing that you are already familiar with, you will be able to use Azure Data Factory and Mapping Data Flows to provide your business with analytics that will result in making better business decisions. Many of the patterns and practices in this book can be applied directly to your projects where you are beginning to build cloud-first data projects in Azure. You can use these techniques to begin building a new set of reusable common ETL patterns. As you work your way through the progression of this book's chapters, you'll build upon the lessons learned in each chapter with the goal of having all of the necessary lessons learned to begin building your own big data analytics ETL solution natively in the cloud using Azure Data Factory with Mapping Data Flows. So welcome, and I hope you find this book helpful as you begin building powerful ETL solutions in the cloud!

PART I

Getting Started with Azure Data Factory and Mapping Data Flows

CHAPTER 1

ETL for the Cloud Data Engineer

In the modern business data ecosystem, "digital transformation" is one of the most prominently used terms to describe the transformation of traditional technology practices to cloud and big data approaches. The term has become a ubiquitous term in IT and has come to represent the embrace of cloud and big data technologies in the data engineering world.

The data part of this digital business transformation puts data engineers at the center of the data processing value chain. What data engineers are challenged with is how to find a way to effectively extract, transform, and load massive amounts of new data points that are often unwieldy in nature. That means that we have to update our ETL processes to meet these new cloud-first big data approaches. Digital transformation is crucial for the success of businesses to compete and grow in today's cloud-first IT strategies, so let's dig into how to adjust and build comparable solutions in Azure using ADF and Mapping Data Flows.

General ETL Process

Figure 1-1 is an example of a general ETL process from traditional on-premises projects where your sources are highly governed source data like data that originates from SAP, database tables, and file extracts that abide by well-known contracts.

© Mark Kromer 2022
M. Kromer, *Mapping Data Flows in Azure Data Factory*, https://doi.org/10.1007/978-1-4842-8612-8_1

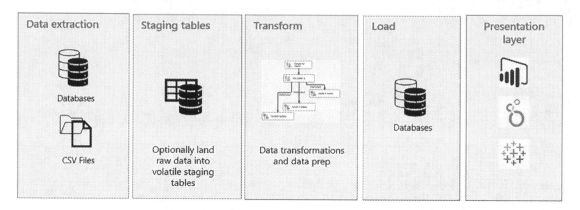

Figure 1-1. *Traditional ETL general process*

As a data engineer working on cloud-first projects in Microsoft Azure, you'll employ a process similar to the diagram in Figure 1-2, which only differs slightly from the concepts shown in Figure 1-1. But the details in each step bring about a significant amount of change that will be the topic of the ADF-specific chapters to come. At the end of the day, the objective of preparing data for business decision makers, who will use business intelligence tools, SQL queries, Excel, data science tools, and other decision-oriented tooling, is no different than you see in traditional on-premises scenarios with highly curated data sources and targets.

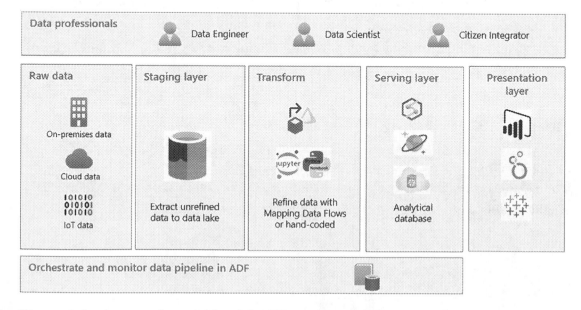

Figure 1-2. *A general example of the ETL process in Azure*

The consumers of the analytics in both of these instances are analysts who are building reports where actual business value is derived for business decision makers. For the data to be useful, the data engineers, data scientists, and citizen data integrators must contribute in a governed way to refining raw data into business-friendly models for exploration and reporting.

Differences in Cloud-Based ETL

We'll need to have a common understanding of what we are achieving in this book, so let's dive into this process in detail and identify some of the differences in cloud-based ETL in Azure from similar traditional on-premises ETL projects:

1. Raw data

    a. Much of the data extraction in big data cloud ETL will be of unknown quality and can change shape and size dramatically between job executions. In ADF, we'll make use of the Copy Activity and Data Flow Activity connectors, linked services, and datasets. In traditional data warehouse scenarios, you may have found that all of your business data resides on-premises and inside the network confines of your business. Additionally, often that data has been curated and already refined through a data quality process. Do not make such assumptions about data that you'll land in the data lake. The details of the different ADF components will come in the next set of chapters.

2. Staging layer

    a. This is where we will land an initial snapshot, lightly transformed, version of the source data in a landing zone in the data lake. For most of the demo scenarios in the book, we'll land the data in Azure Data Lake Store Gen2 (ADLS Gen2 or simply ADLS). If you've previously designed data warehouses with an ODS model or used database tables as staging tables, you can equate the staging layer in the data lake as an analogy. Because the data volumes are expected to be very large here, we will implement incremental data loading patterns in ADF rather than attempt to extract the entire set of data every time.

3. Transform

   a. This is where we will spend a lot of our time and attention in this book using the code-free Mapping Data Flows feature in ADF. We'll build data flows that will perform all different types of data transformations to prepare the data for consumption by our target users. We'll derive columns, aggregate data, and design slowly changing dimension handlers and many more exciting data transformations. A key difference you may find in the transformation layer from traditional ETL projects is that the data will not always be tabular and relational in shape. Rather than expecting to receive database table connections and CSV files, we will need to work with big data native file formats like Parquet, Avro, JSON, and ORC. That can make transformations tricky when you begin to work with arrays, maps, structures, and hierarchies.

4. Serving layer

   a. The serving layer is going to be a data store that is generally a database like Azure SQL Database or Cosmos DB. You will also often use an analytical database like Azure Synapse, Snowflake, or other database targets. Another option here is to simply leave the data in ADLS but utilize Delta Lake folders as a way to organize your data and provide CRUD operations on your analytical data. We'll talk about all of these options in the book including the benefits of both in terms of cost and effectiveness for consumption by business users.

5. Presentation layer

   a. As mentioned earlier, this is where the business users live and how they will access the refined data to make business decisions. Business intelligence tools will utilize the resulting models from the ETL process and create reports and dashboards. The end-user interaction with the resulting data does not change dramatically with modern data approaches to ETL. However, you should keep the requirements in mind in terms of what BI tools will be used. Not all BI tools and business-decision tools can read and work with data in the lake or data stored in formats like Parquet and Delta Lake.

6. Orchestrate and monitor data pipelines in ADF

    a. When thinking about a scalable framework to build and manage complex ETL jobs, it is critical to consider operationalization requirements. In this diagram, I particularly call out orchestration of the pipelines and monitoring of the pipelines. The orchestration piece is not specific just to ADF, but I will only reference ADF techniques in this book. There are many underlying facilities to orchestration that we'll need to touch on that are very important. For example, scheduling jobs, managing the software development life cycle, version control, CI/CD, and more that we'll dive into in later chapters. With common legacy ETL tools, you should already have most of these capabilities. I believe, however, that providing a level of governance to the big data cloud world is even more important because the modern data estate environment can be much more complex than traditional environments. After your pipelines have been scheduled, you need a mechanism to monitor the health of your ETL jobs. We'll walk through setting up alerts and day-to-day monitoring of tasks in ADF later.

Let's dig into each area of the ETL process, starting with the raw data. In modern big data cloud-first data ecosystems, raw data is going to be quite varied and will range from traditional relational database tables with well-defined schemas to raw JSON files with changing properties. You should always expect the unexpected and design your data extraction logic defensively. You may choose to tell ADF to fail your pipeline when attributes or data domains are not within a specified set of constraints. Or you can utilize the built-in concepts of "schema drift" and "data drift" to create a more resilient pipeline that evolves with changing source data. Schema drift occurs when the expected data schema evolves unexpectedly by adding new columns, removing columns, or changing columns. In ADF, you can switch on schema drift handling very easily, and that will tell ADF to accept new or evolving columns. This handling of evolving source data creates a very resilient pattern where your ETL processes will not fail because new columns have been detected. However, it can also hide underlying issues with the source data that you may wish to tag as data quality errors. You will need to make that architectural decision to either fail when the incoming schema breaks the existing contract or continue processing.

Data Drift

Similar to metadata schema drift, data drift occurs when values inside of existing columns begin to arrive outside of a set domain or boundaries. In ADF, you can establish "Assert" expectations that define data ranges. When those domains or ranges of metadata rules are breached in the data, you can fail the job or tag the rows as data quality errors and make downstream decisions on how to handle those errors. For example, you can decide to output an alert, redirect the rows to an error log, or simply ignore the failures and continue processing.

The staging layer is where you will land data from sources into the data lake. In the past, you may have used temporary tables in a database as the staging area, where you would quickly land raw data without transformation. Within Azure, we're going to use ADLS Gen2 using that same analogy of staging data. You are going to land your data into ADLS "Containers," which is where you'll define your folder strategy. In big data storage, folders are very important because they can be used by runtimes like Spark to define file partition strategies. A very common methodology to employ is to create folders based on dates. For example, create a folder structure like this to store raw data of employee data:

```
MyContainer/RawData/Emp/YYYY/YYYYMM.
```

The format of that folder structure inside of your Azure Data Lake would look like Figure 1-3.

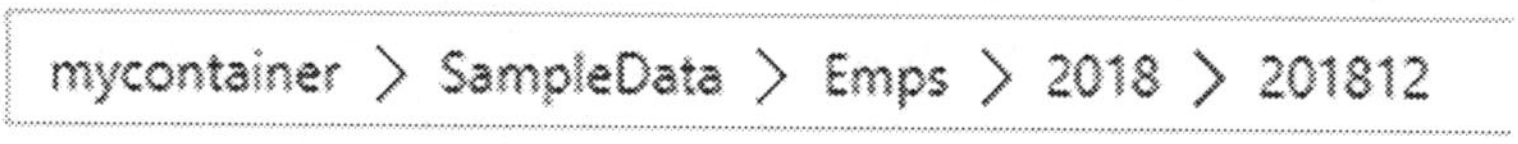

mycontainer > SampleData > Emps > 2018 > 201812

Figure 1-3. *Example folder structure*

Folder partitioning can help with carving out portions of the lake for incremental processing and for partition elimination at query time, improving performance of the Spark engine, which is the execution engine that we'll use in ADF for data transformation. Another common method to optimize your data lake folders for processing is to use key/value pairs to store unique values in your data as folders with data residing in the leaf-level Parquet file as in Figure 1-4.

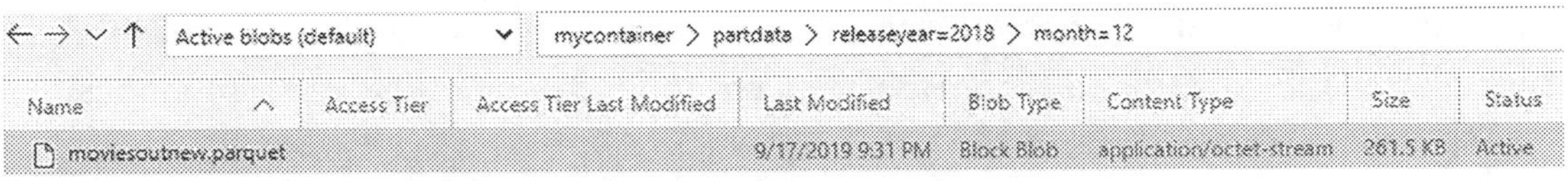
Active blobs (default)
mycontainer > partdata > releaseyear=2018 > month=12
Name
Access Tier
Access Tier Last Modified
Last Modified
Blob Type
Content Type
Size
Status
moviesoutnew.parquet
9/17/2019 9:31 PM
Block Blob
application/octet-stream
261.5 KB
Active

Figure 1-4. *Key value folder partitioning*

In the earlier example, my output data contains the columns "releaseyear" and "month". I've created a folder for every unique "releaseyear" and every unique "month" value in my data using the format of `releaseyear=yyyy/month=mm`. The files residing at the leaf level in that folder structure is Parquet format and, in this particular example, has a friendly name of `moviesoutnew.parquet`. But you cannot assume that files written by ADF and Spark, generally, are going to use readable names like that. In fact, in most cases, it is much more optimal to allow Spark to write the file name based on the job process ID. Don't be surprised to find many files with GUID names in your folders after executing your data pipelines. Throughout this book, we'll use samples that will output partitioned Parquet folders, and we'll configure ADF to automatically create that folder structure.

The transform layer is the topic we'll focus on in depth in the coming chapters. This is where your data transformation logic will reside. In later chapters, we'll design code-free graphs that will perform common ETL operations like slowly changing dimensions, data cleansing, aggregations, fact loading, and data preparation. Those patterns are common throughout the history of ETL and data engineering that we'll update for the modern data landscape. In this book, we'll touch on data partitioning strategies, pushdown optimizations, cluster distributions, and other topics specific to big data in the cloud, including making use of Parquet data formats. Parquet is a columnar, highly compressed file format that is very efficient when used for analytics with Spark, and you'll come across this format throughout the book. But for the purposes of ETL in ADF Mapping Data Flows, assume Parquet will be your default format you'll land your data results as in the lake when using ADF Mapping Data Flows.

Landing the Refined Data

Now that your data has been prepped, cleaned, and transformed, you will land the refined data into an analytical data store to make it available to your end users. This is known as serving layer (not server layer), and typically a database is utilized in this layer as the data store. The biggest change here is that the traditional relational database may be replaced by a cloud-first database, a NoSQL data store, or even just files in the lake. This is where the partitioned Parquet folder techniques listed earlier come into focus. The serving layer can remain a data lake with a computation engine (likely SQL based) serving queries to the presentation layer.

Now that all of the hard work of the data engineer is complete and the ETL project has been established, we reach the top of the analytics value chain: the presentation layer. The data engineer has successfully performed the ETL process of refining raw data into consumable business data for decision makers and analysts, who will utilize tools like Power BI, Excel, Looker, etc., to build reports and dashboards with business metrics and KPIs. Another important audience for analytics in these scenarios will be data scientist. They may use tools to build data models, additional data wrangling, and data exploration using Jupyter Notebooks, SQL queries, or data wrangling tools. Both are target personas for the analytics that you have generated from your ETL jobs.

Typical SDLC

Let's take a look at what the software development life cycle (SDLC) looks like for a typical ETL project with ADF in Figure 1-5.

| Gather business requirements | Design ETL pipelines in new Git branch | Unit test, debug, User acceptance test | Publish to Main branch | Operationalize & monitor |

Figure 1-5. *SDLC for ADF ETL pipeline projects*

We'll walk through configurations needed to connect your data factory to Azure DevOps for Git support in later chapters. But for this conceptual discussion, just focus on the distinct steps that you should follow to produce quality ETL jobs that meet your user requirements.

1. Gather business requirements.

   a. Where do you start with an ETL project? Start by talking with your end users, the business analysts, and data scientists represented in the presentation layer earlier. Essentially, you'll want to deeply understand the consumers of your refined data results and understand the analytics that they need to drive the business with their reports. Ask what data is important to making the right decisions and building the best models. Discuss ways to aggregate complex data and summarize it into business semantics. Then begin tracking down the sources of the data points you'll need to lock to provide the results they're looking for. This exercise should result in a list of required data for your ETL jobs to produce as well as a list of the data sources and access credentials required to get to the source data. Once you've listed all of the sources required and the analytical results you need to produce, you're ready to start designing.

2. Design ETL pipelines in new Git branch.

    a. We'll walk through building a new branch in Git from ADF later. But you can think of this as your first step on a new ADF project. You'll work from a new branch as your sandbox environment. Never develop new pipelines against the live ADF service or from an existing branch. You risk losing work and damaging existing, working code. Now this is where the fun begins! We'll talk in detail soon about how to build code-free graphs for data transformation pipelines.

3. Unit test, debug, user acceptance testing.

    a. Testing your pipelines before release to your production factory is a critical element in an ETL project. It is also another great reason to leverage Git in your ADF project so that you can have a factory that is in a separate development branch, making it much easier to test before deploying to production. We'll talk about testing strategies, debugging, previewing results, and other important factors in this step.

4. Publish from main branch.

    a. After all tests have passed, your next step is to deploy your new pipelines to production. You'll merge your current development branch into a collaboration branch and publish the updates to the live ADF service from your main branch.

5. Operationalize and monitor.

    a. The last set of operations to undertake will include setting a schedule for your pipeline and monitoring the results. We'll walk through different types of schedules that most effectively meet the update cadence uncovered by your business requirements step. Then we'll set alerts for pipeline failures and check the status of our ETL jobs over time.

Summary

We began our journey by learning the fundamentals of ETL in the cloud for data engineers with Azure Data Factory's Mapping Data Flows. Now that we have a clear understanding of the ETL process in Azure, let's begin diving into Azure Data Factory and apply these principles to our first factory.

CHAPTER 2

Introduction to Azure Data Factory

Azure Data Factory is the Microsoft Azure cloud service for data engineers for building, scheduling, and executing data integration and extract, transform, and load (ETL) processes. In this chapter, we'll focus on how to build cloud-first ETL projects using ADF with ADF's Mapping Data Flows code-free data transformation features.

What Is Azure Data Factory?

But first we need to start with a fundamental overview of the ADF service and its components. It is important to have an understanding first of the ADF UI before we begin. You will need to first have an Azure subscription and follow the steps needed to create a new data factory from the Azure portal. We'll walk through those steps at the end of the book when we create a sample project. For now, let's start by looking at the primary high-level concepts in ADF and become a bit more familiar with the pipeline designer as shown in Figure 2-1.

© Mark Kromer 2022
M. Kromer, *Mapping Data Flows in Azure Data Factory*, https://doi.org/10.1007/978-1-4842-8612-8_2

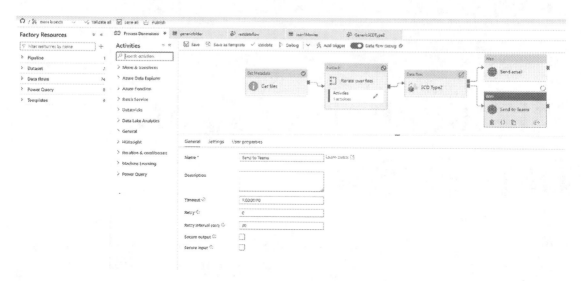

Figure 2-1.   *The ADF web-based user interface*

Let's dig into each one of these high-level concepts in more detail. Figure 2-2 introduces you to each of the data factory resources, which will be described next.

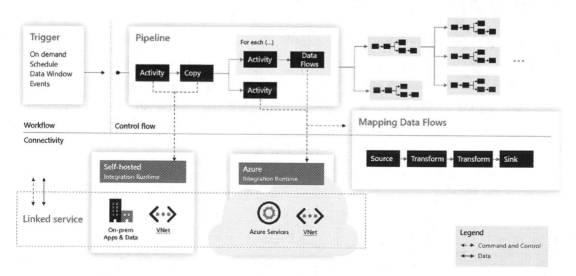

Figure 2-2.   *Azure Data Factory concepts*

Factory Resources

The resource explorer on the far left of the ADF UI represents a list of each of the top-level artifacts in an ADF factory. We're going to skip over discussions of the Power Query and Templates high-level artifacts in this book. Instead, let's talk a bit about each of the primary ADF artifacts that are important for building ETL jobs.

Pipelines

The primary unit of work in ADF is pipelines. Pipelines drive all of the actions that your data integration and ETL jobs perform. A pipeline is essentially a collection of activities that you connect together in a meaningful pattern to create a workflow. All actions in ADF are scheduled through a pipeline execution, including the Mapping Data Flows that we'll build in this book.

Activities

Pipelines are constructed from individual activities. Activities define the individual action that you wish to perform. There are many activities that you can use to compose a pipeline. Examples of activities include copying data (Copy activity), transforming data (Mapping Data Flows), "For Each," "If Then," and other control flow activities. You can also call out to external compute activities like Databricks Notebook and Azure Functions to execute custom code. For this book, we're going to focus on the data flow activity and building Mapping Data Flows for ETL jobs.

Triggers

Triggers allow you to set the conditions for your pipeline to execute. You can create schedule triggers, tumbling window, storage events, and custom events. The most common is schedule triggers, which allow you to set the execute frequency and times for your pipeline trigger. Tumbling window allows for time intervals. ADF will establish windows of time for the recurrence that you choose starting on the date that you choose. Storage events will allow you to trigger your pipeline when a file arrives or is deleted from a storage account. And the final type is custom event triggers.

You can create custom topics in Azure Event Grid and then subscribe to those events. When a specific event is received by your custom event trigger, your pipeline will be triggered automatically.

Mapping Data Flows

This is the code-free data transformation feature that we'll focus on for the rest of this book. Mapping Data Flows has its own browser designer that will open when you create a new data flow. This is where we'll design data transformation graphs and then execute the data flow from a pipeline. You execute your data flow from a pipeline by adding the data flow activity to your pipeline and then choose which data flow to execute.

Linked Services

You will use linked services to store credentials, location, and authentication mechanisms to connect to your data. Linked services are used by datasets and activities in ADF pipelines so that it can be determined where and how to connect to your data. You can share linked service definitions across objects in your factory.

Datasets

Datasets define the shape of your data. In ADF, datasets do not contain or hold any data. Instead, they point to the data and provide ADF information about the schema for your data. In ADF, your data does not require schema. You can work with data in a schema-less manner. When you build ETL jobs using schema-less datasets, you will build data flows that are known as "late binding" and working with "schema drift." It is a very powerful and flexible concept that we'll talk about later and means that your dataset is not required to hold a specific schema at all.

Azure Integration Runtime

Throughout the book, I'll refer to the Azure Integration Runtime as the Azure IR or sometimes simply as IR. This is a configuration object stored in the ADF metastore that defines the location and type of compute that you'll use for parts of your pipeline that require computation. This can mean VMs for copying data, executing SSIS (SQL Server Integration Services) packages, or cluster size and type for Mapping Data Flows. We're not going to talk about SSIS in this book, but it is a very powerful feature in ADF. Basically, you can take your existing SSIS packages from SQL Server and execute them in the cloud using an ADF pipeline. The SSIS Integration Runtime provides the SSIS compute on VMs in a fully managed environment.

The Azure IR also has a Vnet option that allows you to execute your pipelines using compute resources that are inside protected networks. This is a very good option if you are working in a highly regulated industry or your corporate network policies require all services to be Vnets. ADF is a fully managed platform-as-a-service (PaaS) offering, so you do not manage any servers. Since the integration runtimes are the mechanism defining the compute you wish to use for pipeline and data flow execution, this is where you can specify that you need to execute in a protected network. Mapping Data Flows, where we will spend a lot of time digging into in this book, execute on the Spark compute that you specify in the Azure IR. When we get to building our first pipeline with data flows, we'll talk about optimizations and details of the IR.

The Azure IR is a fully serverless managed microservice inside ADF that runs in the cloud. However, you can also configure the networking to connect to your on-premises data sources by peering your network to the Vnet created for your Azure IR. When executing data flow activities in an ADF pipeline, you can use that technique if your data is not in the cloud and not in Azure.

Self-Hosted Integration Runtime

Another approach to executing ADF pipeline activities in a private network or to connect to on-premises data is by using the self-hosted integration runtime or SHIR. This is a software download that you will install on-premises or on a virtual machine that has visibility to your data. ADF will communicate with the SHIR in order to provide access to data in your data center. Self-hosted IR is not supported by Mapping Data Flows, so instead, you'll use the Vnet option in the Azure IR mentioned earlier. Management of all IRs is located in the manage section of the ADF UI left-hand navigation panel (see Figure 2-3).

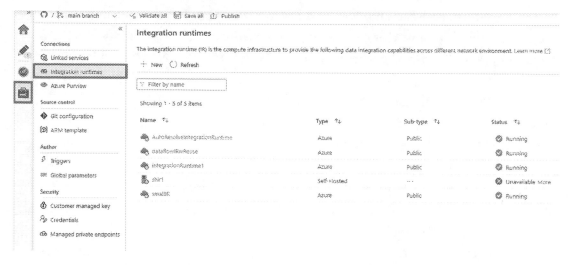

Figure 2-3. *Management screen for Integration Runtimes*

Elements of a Pipeline

The ADF pipeline is the most fundamentally important artifact in your factory, so let's dig into a pipeline first. In Figure 2-4, you'll see an example of a very simple pipeline. It is made up of five activities each interconnected with directional edges in green. The Data Flow activity has both a green and red connector emanating from it. ADF will take the red path if there is a failure from the result of the activity execution, and the green path signifies success. The flow of execution in an ADF pipeline is left to right. If you add activities without connecting lines, those disconnected activities will execute in parallel at the same time as the first node in your connected graph.

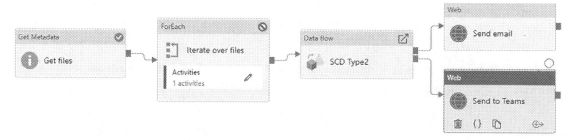

Figure 2-4. *Sample ADF pipeline*

This sample is a pipeline that will call a data flow to process type 2 slowly changing dimensions (SCDs) in a for each loop. The get metadata activity at the start of the pipeline is using a dataset called "genericfolder" (Figure 2-5). This dataset points to a folder in my Azure Blob Store and will loop through each of the files to process different files for each dimension in the target analytical model.

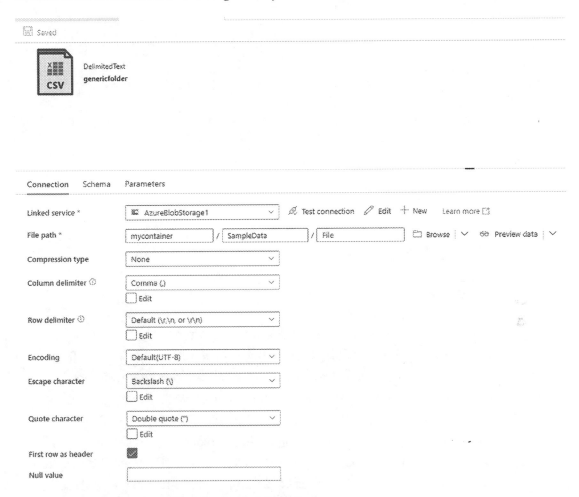

Figure 2-5. *Dataset called "genericfolder"*

The definition of the blob storage account is stored in the Linked Service property of the dataset. In the linked service settings, you set the authentication method and provide credentials for the dataset to use when connecting to your data. In my example, "AzureBlobStorage1", I'm using the account key authentication method in the linked service (see Figure 2-6).

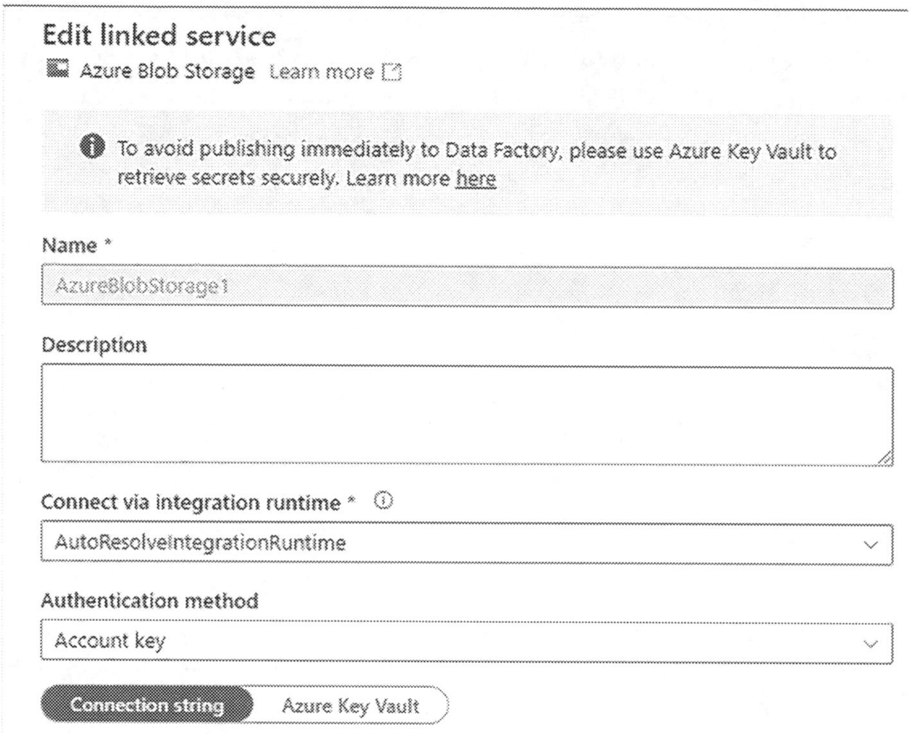

Figure 2-6. *Linked service*

Note that in the dataset "genericfolder" in Figure 2-5, I am pointing to a folder in my blob store located at `mycontainer/SampleData`. This will tell ADF to find all files in that folder and return the list to the get metadata activity. That metadata will now be available to the next activity in the pipeline, which is a For Each activity.

The For Each iterates over each item in a collection. In this case, the collection will be the list of files found in the folder from the get metadata activity. To set an iterator inside the For Each, reference the name of the for each activity and access the `output.childItems` array from the activity: `@activity('Get files').output.childItems`. That will contain the list of files from the dataset folder.

The formulas you write in the ADF pipeline expression editor are known as pipeline expression language (`https://docs.microsoft.com/azure/data-factory/control-flow-expression-language-functions`). To enter expressions, click on the "Add dynamic content" link next to properties and fields in the ADF pipeline designer that allows for custom expressions. The expression editor will slide in (see Figure 2-7), which is where you can enter your expression. To enter the earlier expression for the for each iterator, click on Settings ➤ Items in the get metadata activity settings panel.

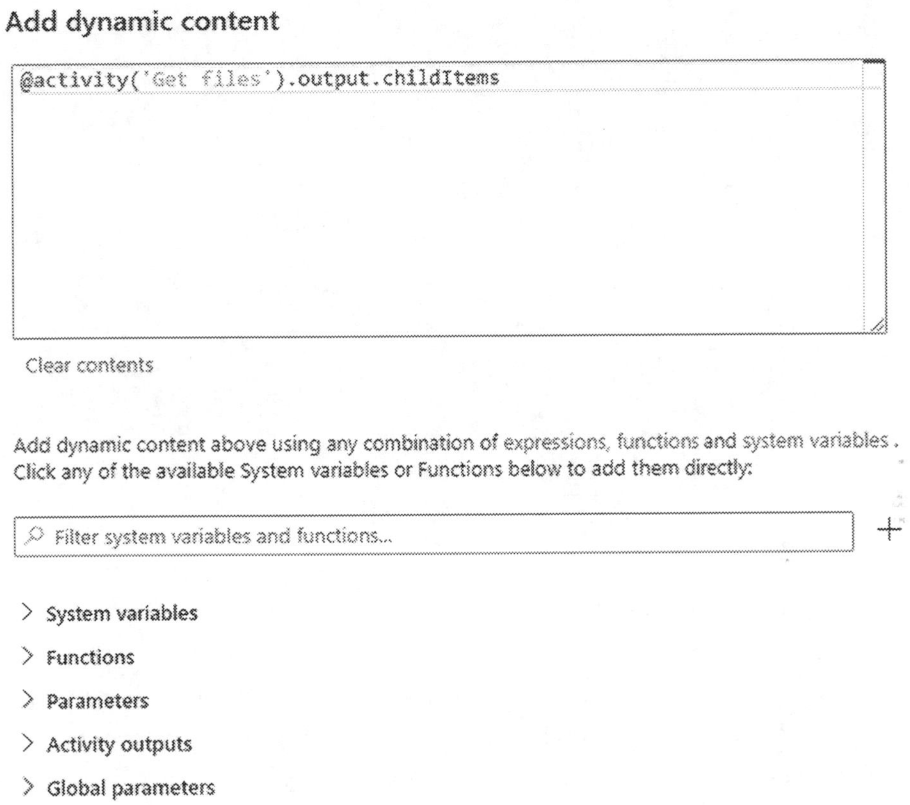

Add dynamic content

```
@activity('Get files').output.childItems
```

Clear contents

Add dynamic content above using any combination of expressions, functions and system variables .
Click any of the available System variables or Functions below to add them directly:

🔍 Filter system variables and functions...   ＋

> System variables

> Functions

> Parameters

> Activity outputs

> Global parameters

Figure 2-7. *Pipeline expression editor*

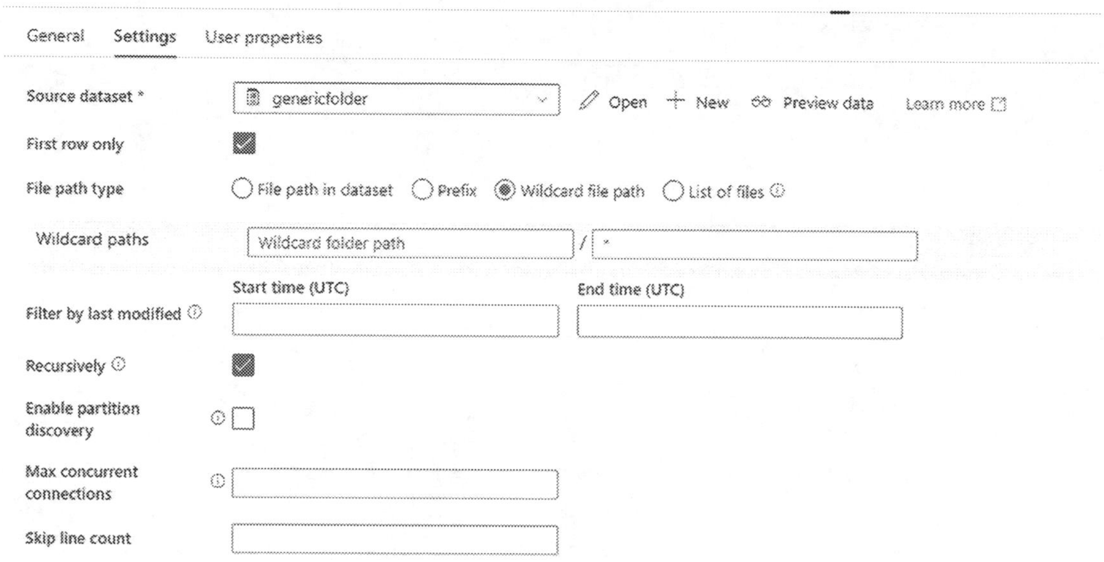

General   **Settings**   User properties

Source dataset *	genericfolder ✎ Open + New ∞ Preview data Learn more ☐
First row only	☑
File path type	○ File path in dataset ○ Prefix ◉ Wildcard file path ○ List of files ⓘ
Wildcard paths	Wildcard folder path / *
Filter by last modified ⓘ	Start time (UTC) End time (UTC)
Recursively ⓘ	☑
Enable partition discovery	ⓘ ☐
Max concurrent connections	ⓘ
Skip line count	

Figure 2-8. *Get metadata settings*

Now that the For Each is connected to the get metadata activity (Figure 2-8), you can add activities inside of the for each. The activities will execute one time for each item in the list. Inside of the for each is a data flow activity (Figure 2-9) that executes the first of two Mapping Data Flows. This first data flow will clean and prep the data from each of the files. You'll learn how to build data cleaning, data quality, and data prep data flows later in this book. To add activities to the For Each, you can double-click on the node in the pipeline graph.

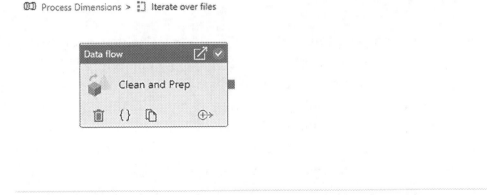

Figure 2-9. *The data flow activity is inside the "for each" iterator activity*

This data flow takes advantage of a very important concept in ADF: parameters. Parameterization allows you to build very flexible and reusable patterns. In this case, the data flow will be passed the parameter of the current item in the iterator by setting this pipeline expression for the data flow activity parameter: @item().name. Parameters are available in most ADF objects including pipelines, datasets, data flows, and linked services. We will make use of parameters later in the book.

Once each file has been cleaned and prepped, this pipeline executes a second data flow activity called "SCD Type 2." We'll talk about slowly changing dimension patterns later. For now, assume that this activity will process each file into each target dimension table.

The final set of activities are web activities. The web activity on the top row is connected to the green or success path from the previous data flow. The second web activity is connected to the red or failure path. This way, we can send success messages to emails and fail messages to Teams.

Pipeline Execution

Once your pipeline is complete, you should test it using the "debug" button on the ADF UI. This will execute your pipeline in a "sandbox" environment as is once your click the button. It is a best practice to configure a Git repo for your factory before developing in ADF. We'll walk through an example of doing that in the final project in this book. For now, we are connected directly to the live factory, so you will not see a connection to a Git repo and you only see a Publish button. Once you have Git enabled, the Save button will light up, and you will publish after your tests have passed.

Once the debug button is pressed (you do not need to publish first), the pipeline is executed in a sandbox test environment. The bottom panel called "Output" will give you live monitoring as your pipeline is being processed (see Figure 2-10). After you've operationalized your pipeline, you will monitor the triggered executions from the pipeline monitoring view using the left-hand navigation icon for monitoring.

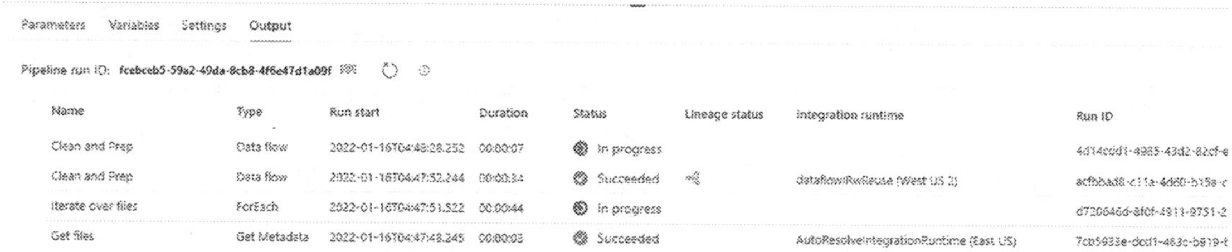

Figure 2-10. *Live monitoring output of debugging the pipeline*

Pipeline Triggers

Executing your pipeline using debug is a good way to test the logic of your workflow. Now that everything has been validated, you can publish this pipeline to the live service and apply a trigger. ADF orchestration is batch oriented, so you must set the mechanism to trigger your pipeline. Your options for triggers are schedule, tumbling window, storage events, and custom events. The most common mechanism is the schedule trigger where you can execute the pipeline based on wall clock time. If you require your pipeline to execute when a file arrives or is removed, choose storage events. Tumbling window will establish a set of time windows (i.e., 15 minutes) that ADF will establish from a start time that you choose. Lastly, custom events are useful by connecting the trigger to Azure Event Grid such that when a specified event occurs, it can trigger your pipeline for a more event-based architecture. Triggers can be shared across pipelines inside your factory, and there is a separate monitoring view organized by trigger. An example of creating a new trigger can be seen in Figure 2-11.

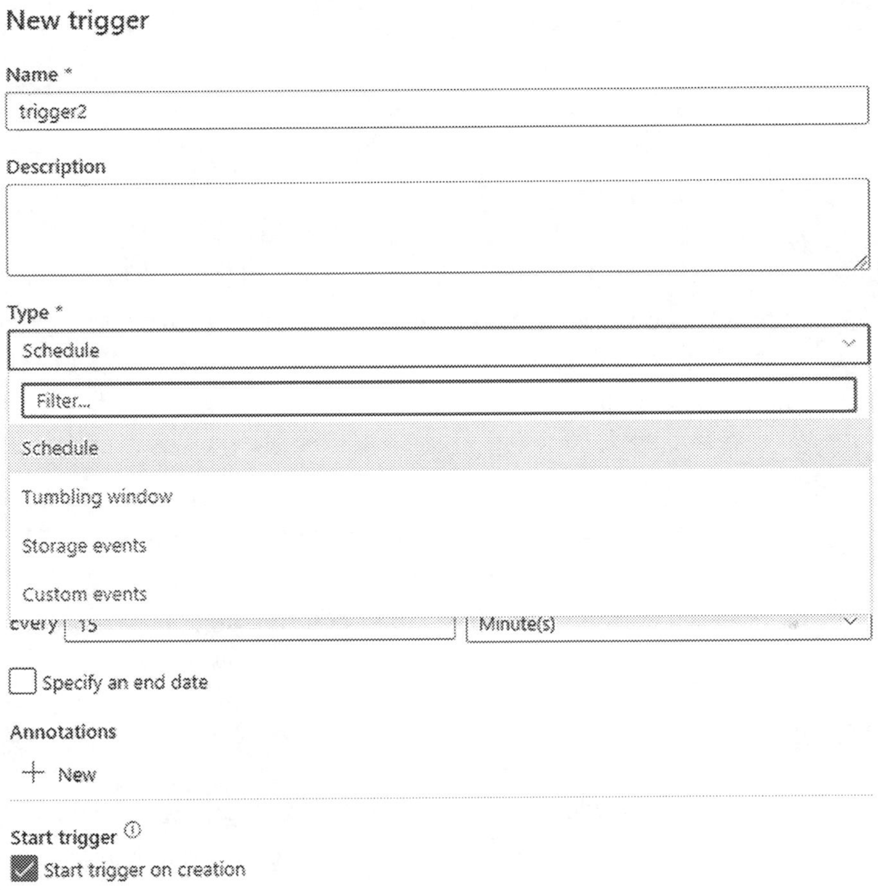

New trigger

Name *

trigger2

Description

Type *

Schedule ∨

Filter...

Schedule

Tumbling window

Storage events

Custom events

every | 15 | Minute(s) ∨

☐ Specify an end date

Annotations

+ New

Start trigger ⓘ
☑ Start trigger on creation

Figure 2-11. *Pipeline trigger*

Pipeline Monitoring

Now that the pipeline design work is completed and tested and a trigger and a schedule have been established, you will want to monitor the progress for success and failure over time. ADF provides live monitoring while debugging and operational debugging from the monitoring view (see Figure 2-12).

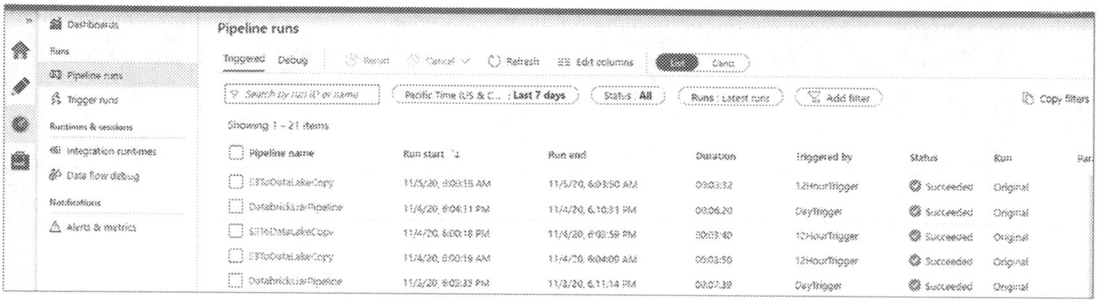

Figure 2-12. *Pipeline monitoring*

Use this view to manage and monitor the health of your factory. The primary view is the pipeline runs view. Clicking into each pipeline on the primary view will provide details of the health and results from each activity. You can further click into each individual activity for details about the execution of each activity. The data flow activity health is very detailed with results that you can track over time to monitor both the health and performance of your ETL jobs. We'll dig deep into monitoring and performance optimizations of data flows later in this book. Other monitoring views include the trigger-based view and health of your integration runtimes. We'll talk more in future chapters specifically about data flow debug monitoring.

Summary

In this chapter, I introduced you to the basic artifacts in ADF, and we looked at a simple example of an ADF pipeline. You've learned the high-level concepts about ADF so that we can begin applying ETL patterns to pipelines using Mapping Data Flows. I demonstrated what a simple pipeline looks like and how to test and publish the workflow for triggered execution. We skipped over many of the detailed workflow options of the pipeline and activities including concurrency, elapsed time metrics, stop points, and rerun so that we can focus instead on ETL patterns. Next, we'll start to dive into building code-free logic for defining ETL jobs.

CHAPTER 3

Introduction to Mapping Data Flows

Mapping Data Flows is the code-free data transformation feature in Azure Data Factory that allows data engineers to build powerful ETL jobs at scale. You can interactively design and test your data flow logic against live data and data samples while constructing a data transformation graph using the Mapping Data Flows designer UI. Then, you can operationalize your work as a Data Flow activity inside of an ADF pipeline. The Azure Integration Runtime is utilized for both debugging and pipeline executions of your data flows, while ADF manages an ephemeral and elastic Spark environment for you in a serverless manner. Throughout the next chapters in this book, I'll refer to the experience of building ETL logic as Mapping Data Flows, the pipeline activity to execute your work as Data Flows, and sometimes will shorten the full name to MDF.

Getting Started

Let's first get familiar with the basics of Mapping Data Flows. In your Data Factory UI, you'll see "Data Flows" as an artifact category under the factory resource explorer on the left. From there (or from the + icon), you can create new data flows (see Figure 3-1). An alternative approach for creating new data flows is from the data flow pipeline activity. You will also see a "+ new" option in the data flow activity when you add the activity to a pipeline.

© Mark Kromer 2022
M. Kromer, *Mapping Data Flows in Azure Data Factory*, https://doi.org/10.1007/978-1-4842-8612-8_3

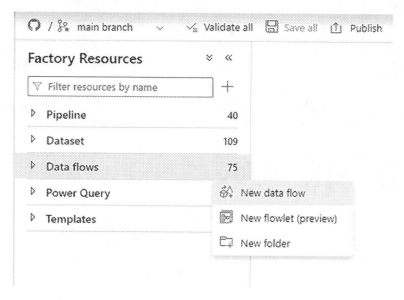

Figure 3-1. *Creating new data flow*

Creating a new data flow will open the Mapping Data Flows design surface with a blank canvas and a blank source transformation (see Figure 3-2). Every data flow must have at least one source and can have multiple sources. It is very common to include many sources inside your data flows as well as many sinks

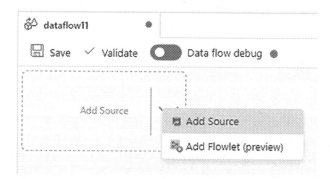

Figure 3-2. *New data flow from the Mapping Data Flow design surface*

When you click the "Add Source" text in the middle of the source transformation, ADF will add a new source, which is the same as clicking the arrow and selecting "Add Source". The default is "Add Source", while "Add Flowlet" allows you to create customized sources that a set of transformation templates. We'll dive into Flowlets as data flow templates a bit later.

Before we talk in detail about building the flow, I'd like to point out the data flow debug button on the top of Figure 3-2. This is an important feature in MDF that you'll use for interactive debugging and testing. Turning the debug session on during your data flow design will start a serverless Spark cluster that is managed by ADF. The size and type of compute used are defined the Azure Integration Runtime (IR). By default, ADF uses the "AutoResolveIntegrationRuntime" for debug sessions. You can choose a different IR when starting your debug session to configure the session to your own requirements. You may need more compute or may have more memory-intense operations that require a more powerful Spark cluster. In Figure 3-3, I am using a custom Azure IR that I created called "dataflowIRwReuse". It uses Memory Optimized compute and has a total of 48 cores, with 32 cores dedicated to Spark worker nodes. The default Azure IR has 8 total cores (4 for a driver and 4 for a worker) and uses general-purpose VMs.

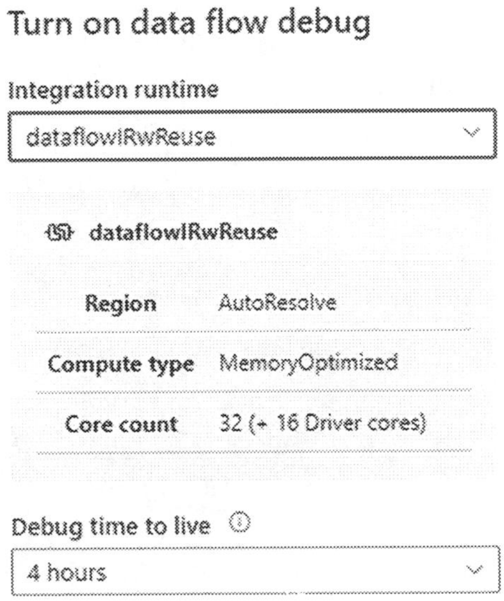

Turn on data flow debug

Integration runtime

| dataflowIRwReuse | ∨ |

🔁 dataflowIRwReuse	
Region	AutoResolve
Compute type	MemoryOptimized
Core count	32 (+ 16 Driver cores)

Debug time to live ⓘ

| 4 hours | ∨ |

Figure 3-3. *Choosing the IR for your debug session*

While you don't need to turn on the debug session to design and build your data flows, you will need it for interactive debugging to view your data throughout each step in the flow. Without the debug session being active, you can still design, build, and view most metadata. There is a section in this chapter dedicated to debugging where we will dive into detail. For now, let's dig into using the design surface to build a graph made up of transformation primitives that you can use to build your data flow graph.

Design Surface

You will construct your data flow from left to right. An example of a completed data flow graph is in Figure 3-4.

You will pick the node on the graph that you wish to add a transformation to by clicking on the plus sign (+) on the preceding transformation node. Clicking the plus sign will launch the transformation toolbar with a palette of transformation primitives (see Figure 3-6). Mapping Data Flows are made up of vertices (transformation nodes) and edges (connector lines). You'll also see the term "stream" representing portions of your data flow. Streams are roughly equivalent to the transformation nodes in your graph. The term is used throughout ADF as a way to describe a step or series of steps in your data flow. Since the visual graph is a UI construct on top of the underlying data flow script (more on this later), the resulting script ordering of your logic may look slightly different from the ordering in your graph. ADF may sometimes rewrite your logic in a way that is more optimal for Spark, resulting in an execution order that does not match your graph's visual ordering. Therefore, we use the term "stream", which describes an arbitrary step in your resulting data flow script that may or may not actually transform data.

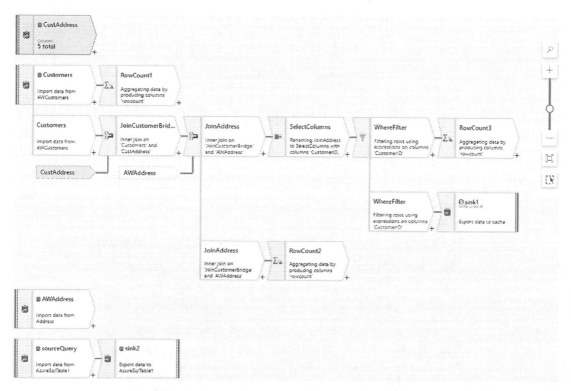

Figure 3-4. *Mapping Data Flows design surface*

Let's talk a bit about a few of the graph constructs that you'll see and work with in Mapping Data Flows. First, it is important to note that a valid data flow must have at least one source and one sink. When you connect your factory to Git, you can save your data flow without a source or sink, but your data flow will not validate. If you are not connected to source control, you can only publish. That means there is no way to save a "scratch" copy. ADF will always validate in live (no Git) mode because it is a publish operation.

When you click on the canvas of the data flow, you will see a bottom panel with parameters and settings. Parameters can be used to pass values into the data flow from the pipeline and utilize those values as reference throughout your logic. The settings tab allows you to set the order in which the sink is written. The order of operations in a data flow is right to left. You set the order that the data is written. Note that the ordering will be grouped by connected graphs. That is, you cannot set the order of each individual sink because sinks that are "connected" are grouped together. A connected graph in your data flow is any part of your logic that is connected by connector lines or reference lines.

Connector Lines and Reference Lines

Every transformation in your graph is connected by a solid horizontal connector line. Although you construct your graph left to right, the ordering of the actions can be grouped by the ADF executor. We'll walk through evaluation of the execution plans a bit later using the ADF monitoring views. That will be the best way to visualize the actual execution of your logic once it is sent to the Spark cluster.

Vertical bars connect transformations that are copies of existing streams. These are drawn automatically for you to indicate the corresponding stream connections. The resulting connection of nodes with connected edges (connector lines) is known as a connected graph in ADF.

Reference lines are used to connect to reference nodes that are used as a way to indicate relationships in joins, lookups, and other transformations using multiple inputs. A reference node and a connector line will be added to the canvas automatically by ADF as a way to avoid drawing confusing and overlapping lines on your graph.

There is a right-click option when you click on the design surface to hide or show reference nodes. This is helpful to show a slightly cleaner view of your graph when you have very complex data flows. To gain more screen real estate on large graphs, you can also use the zoom control to zoom out using smaller vertices (Figure 3-5). As you zoom out, you will lose some detail as a sacrifice for seeing a larger portion of the graph on your viewport.

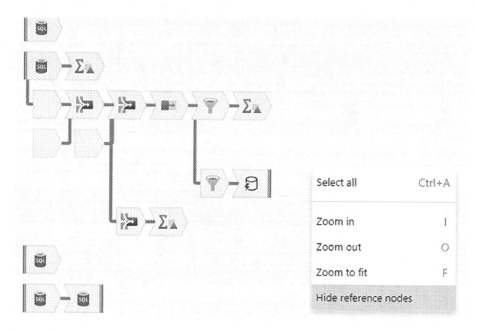

Figure 3-5. *The MDF design surface zoomed out*

Repositioning Nodes

The ADF Mapping Data Flow design surface is a construction paradigm, where you build your logic and ADF will manage the layout for you. However, if you need to move a node, you can do this through configuration. By clicking on the node that you wish to move, you can change the incoming stream to point to a different transformation. This will reposition the node to the location in the graph that you choose in the incoming stream drop-down. Doing this operation may have several side effects that you should be aware of. It will result in a reformatting of your graph, and it can change the downstream metadata depending upon the actions of the transformation that you moved. So you may have to follow up this action with additional cleanup to validate your data flow and graph hygiene. In Figure 3-6, I am demonstrating how you can use the Incoming Stream property on a transformation node to move the graph node to a different location in the graph by connecting it to a different incoming stream.

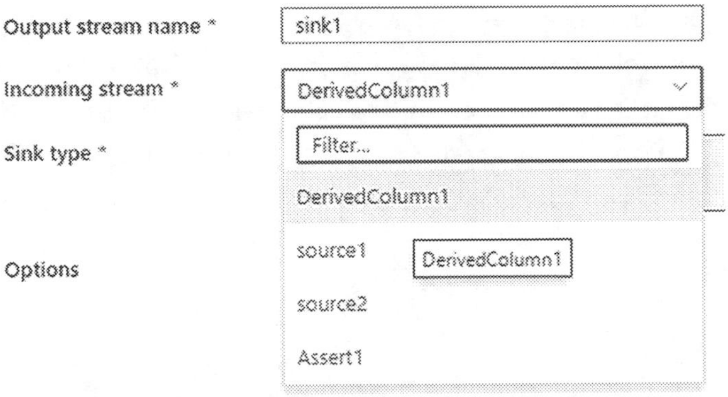

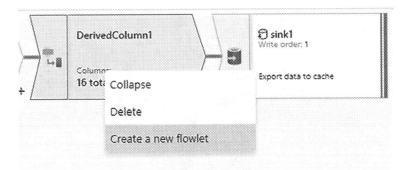

Figure 3-6. *Reconnecting a transformation to a different stream*

There is a right-click action available on each transformation node (Figure 3-7) that you can use to hide the remainder of the graph that is to the right of your current location. Click "Collapse", or alternatively, double-click a node and the remainder of the graph will collapse. You can double-click again or right-click and select "Expand" to expand the collapsed portion of the graph and toggle between collapsed and expanded graph sections.

Figure 3-7. *Graph node right-click actions*

To delete transformation nodes, right-click on the node and select "Delete" or simply select and press the delete keyboard button. Another available action to you is to multiselect nodes with the keyboard shift button and then right-click and select "Create a new Flowlet". That will generate a new object in your factory under the "Data Flows" category, taking that selected portion of your graph and generating a new reusable data flow object called a "Flowlet". We'll talk in more detail later about flowlets and how to use them to create flexible, modular data flow logic. Figure 3-8 is also a screenshot of the right-hand canvas control for zoom and for multiselect. If you turn on multiselect, ADF will allow you to use a lasso control to multiselect portions of your graph for deletion or Flowlet using the left mouse button (Figure 3-9). With multiselect turned off, the left mouse button will allow you to move the graph around on your viewport window.

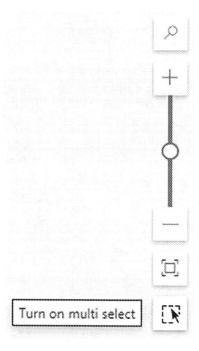

Figure 3-8. *Zoom and multiselect options*

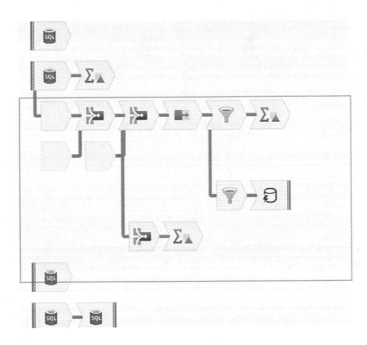

Figure 3-9. *Multiselect box of multiple nodes*

Data Flow Script

The data flow script is the fundamental artifact being generated by ADF's Mapping
Data Flow UI. It is the grammar that describes your data transformation intent that will
be packaged and marshaled to the Spark cluster for compilation and execution. The
underlying serverless Spark cluster that is described in your Azure IR configuration
knows nothing about your data flow graph and will only ever receive the script to
execute. The UI in ADF will fully manage the data flow script. However, you can view and
edit the script manually and generate data flow scripts for use in the ADF SDK to auto-
generate data flow pipelines. To access the script behind your graph, click on the "Script"
button on the top right of the design surface (Figure 3-10). Next to the script button is
the "Code" button. While the script button is unique to the Mapping Data Flows canvas,
the code button is available on all areas of ADF and will show the representative JSON
definition of each object that is being edited. Like the data flow script, the ADF JSON can
also be edited manually through this mechanism.

Figure 3-10. *Data flow script-behind button*

The following code snippet is a simple example of what the script behind the graph will look like. This data flow has a source, aggregate, derived column, and sink transformation. The name of each transformation is after the "~>" syntax. The ordering of the graph nodes is determined by the name of the transformation at the beginning of each new element.

```
source(output(
            medallion as string,
            hack_license as string,
            vendor_id as string,
            rate_code as long,
            store_and_fwd_flag as string,
            pickup_datetime as timestamp,
            dropoff_datetime as timestamp,
            passenger_count as long,
            trip_time_in_secs as long,
            trip_distance as double,
            pickup_longitude as double,
            pickup_latitude as double,
            dropoff_longitude as double,
            dropoff_latitude as double
        ),
        allowSchemaDrift: true,
        validateSchema: false,
        format: 'table') ~> source1
source1 aggregate(groupBy(vendor_id),
        avgDistance = round(avg(trip_distance),2)) ~> Aggregate1
```

```
Aggregate1 derive(vendorFullName = case (vendor_id == 'CMT', 'Mobile
Knowledge Systems',        vendor_id == 'VTS', 'Verifone Transportation
Systems')) ~> DerivedColumn1
DerivedColumn1 sink(allowSchemaDrift: true,
        validateSchema: false,
        recreate:true,
        format: 'table',
        skipDuplicateMapInputs: true,
        skipDuplicateMapOutputs: true) ~> sink1
```

Transformation Primitives

Throughout the book, we'll use the data flow transformation primitives and configure
each of them in interesting ways using the powerful ADF data transformation expression
language. For now, allow me to simply introduce each of the current transformation
primitives (see Figure 3-11). To launch the toolbar, click on the plus sign (+) on any
transformation, or first add a source transformation, and then you'll see the plus sign.

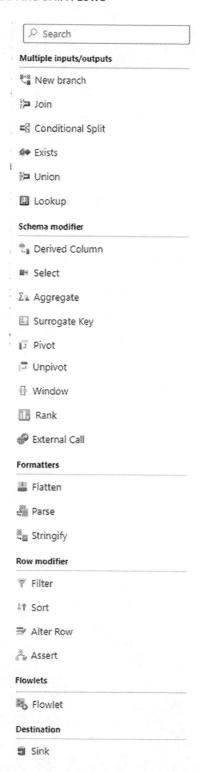

Figure 3-11. *Data flow transformation toolbar palette*

Multiple Inputs/Outputs

This category of transformations takes one or more inputs, and it outputs one or more streams. Let's take a look at the transformations available as multiple inputs and outputs.

New Branch

Use this transformation to duplicate an existing stream. The new stream will not be valid until you add another transformation directly after the new branch. In the design surface, ADF will duplicate the node and will show a connector line between the original and new branch.

Join

Join two streams together using a common SQL join set logic (Figure 3-12). The left stream is the incoming stream from the previous transformation. Set the right stream to whichever step in your flow that you wish to join together. This is very powerful as it allows you to join, merge, and federate data from many different sources.

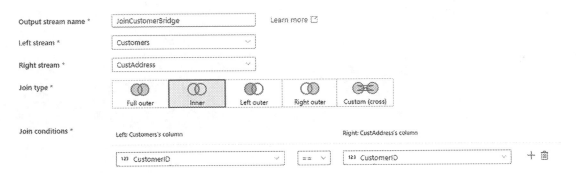

Figure 3-12. *Join transformation*

Conditional Split

Split your data based on a Boolean expression. You set the condition using the expression builder and define a new output stream based on each condition. You can have as many conditions as you need. Think of this as an if/then/else or case statement.

Exists

Check for the existence or nonexistence of values between the incoming stream and another transformation stream. Similar to a SQL Exists statement.

Union

Combine two or more streams together using the "Union with" drop-down to select the streams to union together. You can union the streams based on the column names or based on ordinal position.

Lookup

Lookup is a left outer join that provides additional values to your stream for a real-time refence data lookup (Figure 3-13). If the data you are looking up does not change frequently, then a better performing option will be the cached lookup that uses a cached sink.

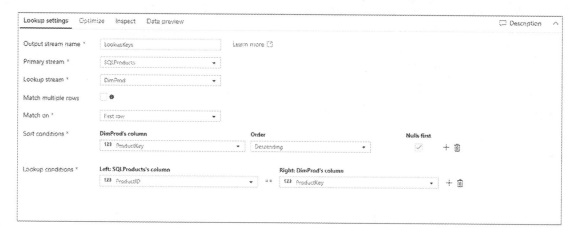

Figure 3-13. *Lookup transformation*

Schema Modifier

Schema modifier transformations will have effect on the output of the shape of your data. You can view the change in the shape of your data using the output tab of the Inspect panel in each transformation.

Derived Column

This is one of the most common transformations that you'll include in your data flows. The derived column allows you to modify existing columns or to create new columns. The values used to define the new or modified columns are based on expression formulas. You'll spend a lot of time inside of derived columns using the expression builder to design your transformation formulas here.

Select

The select transformation is roughly equivalent to a SQL select statement. You will use this transformation to reorder, rename, and reshape your schemas.

Aggregate

Another very common transformation, the aggregate is intended to give you a place to collect values together using an aggregate function in the ADF data flow expression language. You can optionally group by columns or expression here, similar to a SQL aggregate statement. Note that if you do not group values, ADF will have to aggregate across your entire dataset, which can be a blocking operation at runtime that may result in long-running data flows when a lot of data is present.

Surrogate Key

Use the surrogate key transformation to create an incrementing unique key, commonly used in dimension tables.

Pivot

This is a classic pivot function transformation to transform row values into columns.

Unpivot

Transform columns into row values. Very useful when normalizing data and to reshape incoming source data files.

Window

The Window transformation will allow you to utilize all of the window and aggregation functions in the ADF data flows library. The UI requires the typical SQL Window function properties like range, ordering, and window function.

Rank

This is a scaled-out rank function that will perform very well against big data. Both rank and dense rank are supported and are much more scalable than rank() and denseRank() functions using the window transformation.

External Call

If you would like to add to your data from external REST APIs or to call an action from an external REST resource, then use this transformation.

Formatters

The formatters category of transformation focuses on handling complex data formats. These transformations will allow you to define, shape, and deconstruct data that has complex formats.

Flatten

When working with arrays, you can unroll the arrays using the Flatten transformation. Very helpful when you need to convert arrays for tabular output or if you need to perform calculations and transformations on values inside of an array.

Parse

When you have string fields in your data that contain a structure like embedded JSON, XML, or delimited text columns, use the Parse transformation to ask ADF to turn that plain text into the appropriate structures.

Stringify

The inverse transformation of parse is Stringify. This will take a structure like JSON and turn it into plain text for tabular destinations.

Row Modifier

Use row modifier transformations to change the order of rows. You can also use it to set flags on rows based on criteria that you specify.

Filter

Similar to a where clause in a SQL select statement, this will filter out rows from your stream that do not meet the filter condition which you specified.

Sort

You can set the sort order of your data, but I recommend that you only use this for smaller data and very specific purposes. It is a slow operation and a blocking operation because Spark will have to coalesce all of the data into a single partition during execution. It is useful to sort during testing so that you can see specific values and validate your data.

Alter Row

This transformation is how you will set flags on data flows that write to databases. Use it to set row policies that determine if the row should be inserted, updated, deleted, or merged (upsert).

Assert

Assert is a data quality and data validation transformation. You can build your own set of expectations and rules to flag rows as failing your assertions. You will be able to create your own assert ID and description that you can query and output as part of a failed assertion.

Flowlets

Flowlets are a special category by themselves. We will utilize flowlets in this book as a way to create reusable data flow logic in your factory. Think of flowlets as templates that have an input and output contract that you can set to plug your flowlets into different data flows.

Destination

The final transformation we'll cover is the sink. You'll find this in the Destination category in the data flow toolbox. This is what you will use to define the destination for your transformed data. You can also use the sink to store your results in memory in the Spark cluster by setting the sink to a cache. This is useful for cached lookups throughout your data flow and also to pass results back to the calling pipeline.

Expression language

The ADF expression language for transformation in data flows is very powerful and very expressive in terms of building power ETL jobs. Writing expression formulas is basically the most "code" that you'll need to write when defining your data flows. We'll talk in detail about different transformation expression languages throughout the book, so I just wanted to introduce you to the visual concept for now. When you click the link "Open expression builder" or "Add dynamic content" inside of the designer, you will be taken to the expression builder experience (Figure 3-14). You will use the expression box to build and validate your formula. ADF will provide IntelliSense and auto-complete features with inline help to assist you in your formula validation. Enter a new column name or select the column you wish to modify in the top left of the expression builder dialog box. Under expression elements, you will find different categories. Let's talk briefly about these.

Functions

In the Functions category, you will find a list of all of the built-in and user-defined functions in your factory that can be used inside your expressions.

Input Schema

The input schema is the list of columns that are available to you to use in your expressions. This list should look similar to the list of columns in the inspect pane's input. Note that only named columns will appear here. Columns that are not defined in the source transformation's projection or in a transformation column name are considered late-binding or "schema drift." We'll talk later in the book about how to access those hidden fields in transformation expressions.

Parameters

Data flow parameters are used as a way to pass values into your data flow from a pipeline. When you are debugging using data preview in the Mapping Data Flow design surface, you can set parameter values under debug settings.

Cached Lookup

A cached lookup will pull data that is stored in memory in your current data flow. The way to hydrate the cache is to add a sink that is a cached sink. This lookup mechanism is much more performant than the lookup transformation. However, the data can become stale over the lifetime of the data flow, whereas the lookup can retrieve updated values on every lookup.

Locals

This is where you will create and use local variables. Locals are useful if you have complex formulas that you are using more than once inside your transformation. These variables are scoped locally to just the transformation where it was created.

Data Preview

Data preview is available both in the data preview panel in the transformation settings and in the expression builder. The debug session must be turned on for this feature to work. Previewing data using samples is the best mechanism to use for debugging your work while designing.

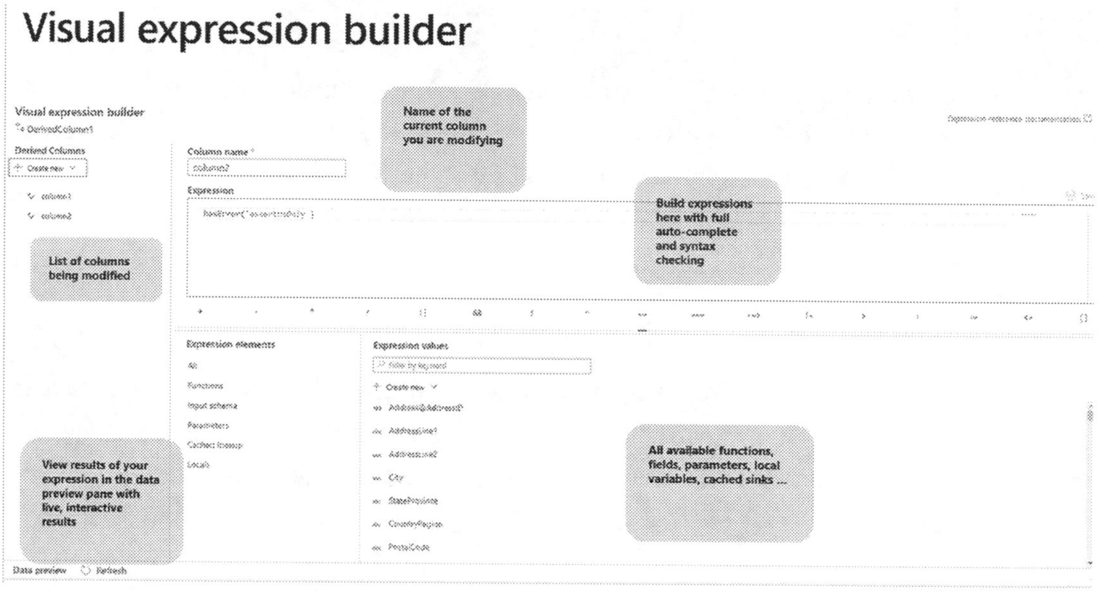

Figure 3-14. The Mapping Data Flows expression builder

Manage Compute Environment from Azure IR

You can access Azure IR settings from the manage icon on the left-hand navigation pane in the ADF UI. Figure 3-4 is an example of the Azure IR configuration panel. There is a radio button to turn on the managed Vnet option for the Azure IR and for the region where you wish to execute your data flows. The default is "auto resolve", which means ADF will spin up the Spark compute in the same region as your factory. You have the option of using a different Azure region for data flow computation. Under the data flow runtime section is where you will select the type of compute, core count, and time to live (TTL). These are Spark cluster configuration settings that define how much compute you wish to use for your data flows. Azure IRs can be applied to each debug session and to each data flow activity in your pipelines. The default is a 4+4 cluster using general-purpose compute. That is a good setting for debugging your first data flows using smaller data samples. As your workloads become larger and more complex, it is recommended to upgrade to a memory-optimized Azure IR and apply more cores as your data grows. The more cores you apply to your Azure IR, the larger the VMs and the more data partitions that Spark can apply to your workloads. The cost of your data flow pipeline is based on core hours. So while a larger-sized Azure IR may have a higher price point, if your pipeline completes in a quicker manner, you may actually end up saving money in the end.

It is also recommended to set a TTL on the IR. The time to live tells ADF to keep the Spark cluster around for that period of time after the completion of the last data flow job. This way, ADF will not have to provision a new cluster, resulting in the three to four-minute latency. The default Azure IR does not have a TTL, so it is a good practice to always create your own named Azure IR with a TTL so that there is no delay in your data flow executions.

For debug sessions, the TTL is set in the dialog in Figure 3-15. The TTL discussed here is solely used for operationalized executions of the data flow activity from a pipeline. For this chapter, we are going to focus on just the interactive mapping design interface.

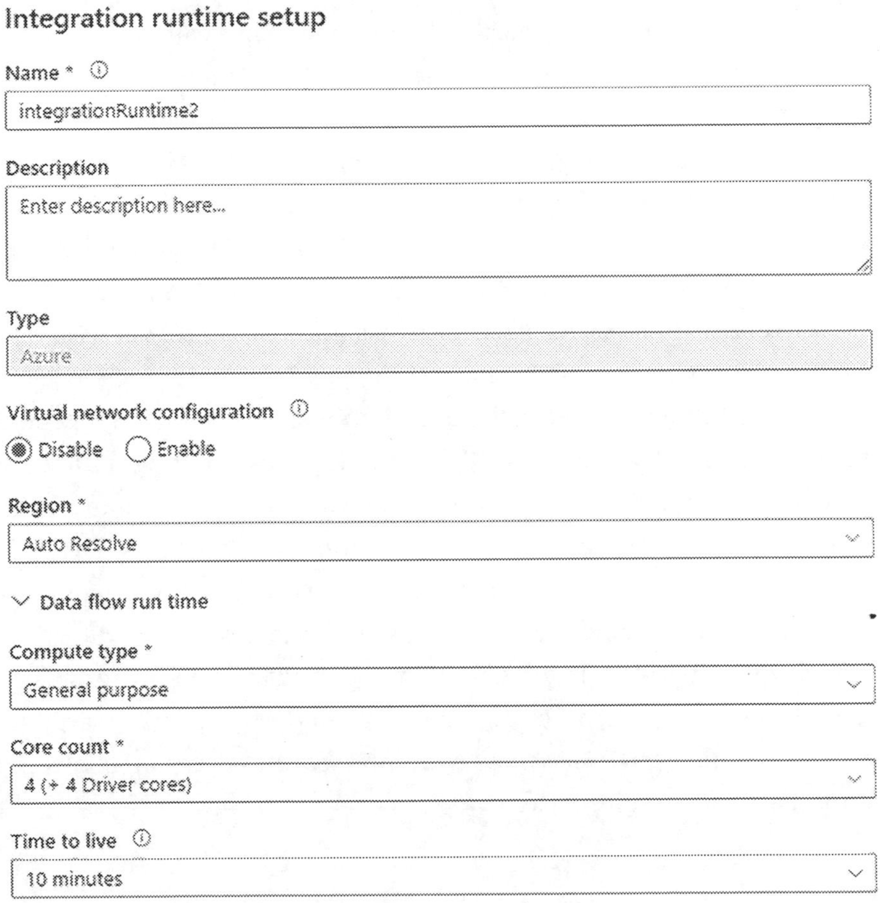

Integration runtime setup

Name * ⓘ

> integrationRuntime2

Description

> Enter description here...

Type

> Azure

Virtual network configuration ⓘ
◉ Disable ◯ Enable

Region *

> Auto Resolve

∨ Data flow run time

Compute type *

> General purpose

Core count *

> 4 (+ 4 Driver cores)

Time to live ⓘ

> 10 minutes

Figure 3-15. Azure Integration Runtime settings

47

Debugging from the Data Flow Surface

Now that you understand the basic transformation primitives, data flow script, and expressions, let's talk a bit about debugging while building your logic. Each node contains a tab in the bottom panel called "Inspect". This will track the metadata being passed and modified throughout your flow. You do not need to have a debug session turned on, as this information is stored in the browser and in the data flow.

However, you should start a debug session so that you can view your data live during design time to see the data change in each step. When starting your debug session, it will take ADF three to four minutes to provision and hydrate a new Spark cluster. That cluster will stay alive for the amount of time you specify in the debug session dialog box in Figure 3-3. Once the cluster is online, the debug session indicator will turn green. Now you can view the results of each of your transformation steps against live data in real time.

The general pattern for debugging while building a data flow is to switch on the debug session, observe the data from the data preview tab in each transformation step, and use the Inspect tab to validate and track your metadata throughout the data flow (Figure 3-16). Data preview in design mode is the most effective way to unit test and stop-point test to ensure that your logic is valid by using samples of data. No data is written to your sink destinations while inside the designer. The data preview in each transformation is a peek at a sample of the data in memory inside the Spark cluster data frames (Figure 3-17). You can adjust the sampling sizes in debug settings, and you can also choose custom queries or use sample data files for your sources for more targeted testing. Those options are also available under debug settings. The default for sampling is 1000 rows in data preview when designing your data flow (Figure 3-18). It is recommended to use sampling during debug so that the design experience can bring back data results quickly. The default Azure IR being used for debugging is a small 8-core cluster, so avoid using large sample sizes. That being said, you can use a larger cluster by choosing an Azure IR that you've assigned with more cores. When you choose a larger IR, you can increase the sampling size.

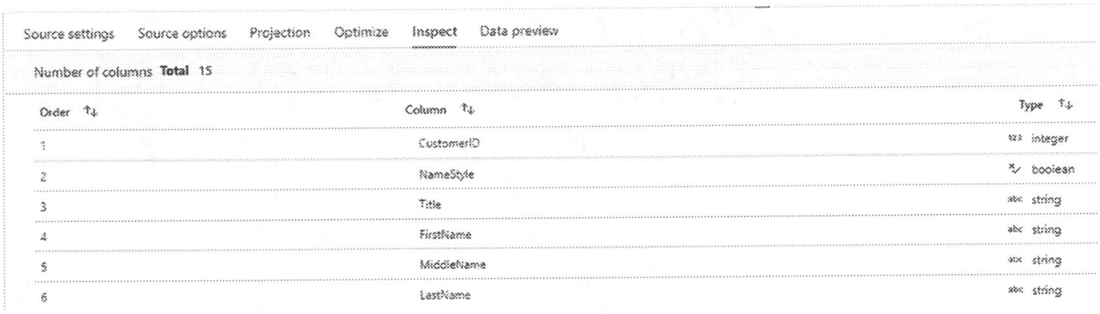

Source settings	Source options	Projection	Optimize	Inspect	Data preview			

Number of columns **Total** 15

Order ↑↓	Column ↑↓	Type ↑↓
1	CustomerID	123 integer
2	NameStyle	boolean
3	Title	abc string
4	FirstName	abc string
5	MiddleName	abc string
6	LastName	abc string

Figure 3-16. *Inspect tab showing column metadata*

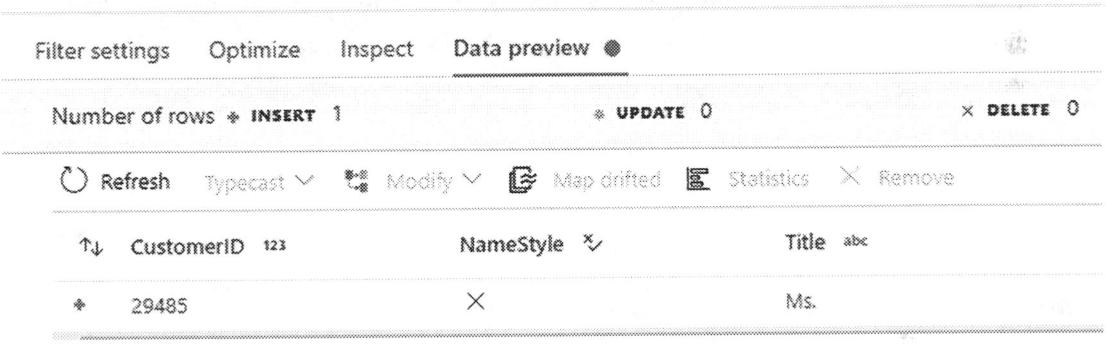

Filter settings	Optimize	Inspect	Data preview ●		

Number of rows   **INSERT** 1   **UPDATE** 0   ✕ **DELETE** 0

◯ Refresh   Typecast ∨   Modify ∨   Map drifted   Statistics   ✕ Remove

↑↓ CustomerID 123	NameStyle	Title abc
✦ 29485	✕	Ms.

Figure 3-17. *Data preview of live data using the debug session*

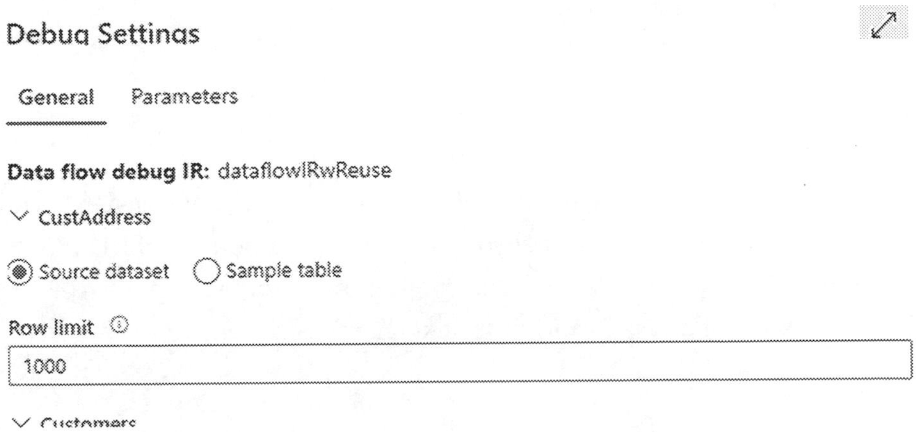

Debug Settings

General   Parameters

Data flow debug IR: dataflowIRwReuse

∨ CustAddress

◉ Source dataset   ◯ Sample table

Row limit ⓘ

1000

∨ Customers

Figure 3-18. *Setting the debug Azure IR*

Debugging from Pipeline

Once everything is fully unit tested from a data preview perspective and you're satisfied with your logic in your flow, you can test your work in a pipeline. Start a new ADF pipeline and add the data flow activity. By testing the logic inside of a pipeline, ADF will use the entire dataset for each source so that you can now test against a larger dataset. Also, when executing from a pipeline, ADF will write data to your sink destinations. You may wish to stepwise increase the amount of data for testing, which you can accomplish by utilizing the sampling option (see Figure 3-19) in each source setting inside your data flow. Keep in mind that this setting will become part of your final pipeline, so be sure to disable sampling prior to deploying the data flow pipeline for production use. The default sampling size in the source is 100. This property is ignored for data preview and only used during pipeline execution.

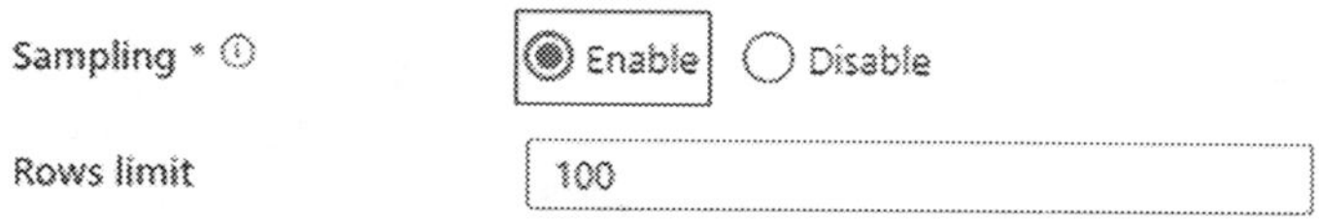

Sampling * ⓘ	◉ Enable	○ Disable
Rows limit	100	

Figure 3-19. Enabling sampling for sources from pipeline run

To test from a pipeline, click on (+) new pipeline from the ADF UI. You can drop and drag the data flow from the data flow category in the resource explorer, or drag and drop the data flow activity from the pipeline toolbox.

Summary

In this chapter, I introduced the basics of ADF's Mapping Data Flows design surface and the debugging experience. Now that you have the fundamentals of ETL, ADF, and Mapping Data Flows, let's put those lessons together by building a practical example of an ADF ETL pipeline using data flows in the next chapter.

PART II

Designing Scalable ETL Jobs with ADF Mapping Data Flows

CHAPTER 4

Build Your First ETL Pipeline in ADF

Azure Data Factory (ADF) is a comprehensive Azure cloud service for data engineers to build complex data integration and ETL data pipelines. In the first few chapters, I've introduced cloud ETL concepts, Azure Data Factory basics, and the Mapping Data Flow design surface. Let's start to put some of these conceptual discussions into concrete project terms. Since the focus of this book is the low-code data transformation feature Mapping Data Flows, we'll take this chapter to walk through what it would take to build your first ADF pipeline that focuses on designing an ETL job using Mapping Data Flows inside an ADF pipeline to achieve a simple data analytics pattern, without writing any code.

Scenario

For this chapter, the scenario we'll center on will be data quality in ETL. As data engineers, we've been tasked with preparing a database table of address transactions for downstream analytics in the data lake. I'm going to use the common AdventureWorks address table (SalesLT.Address) from my Azure SQL Database. You can load this sample data into your Azure SQL server instance from the Azure portal and follow along from your subscription. The requirements for this scenario are that we need to clean the address field in the Address table, filter out non-US addresses, and abbreviate the "CountryRegion" column. Lastly, we'll generate a new computed column (derived column) and call it "Full Address". At the end of the data flow, we'll land the new data as Parquet in ADLS Gen2, a very common pattern in Azure cloud-first ETL.

© Mark Kromer 2022
M. Kromer, *Mapping Data Flows in Azure Data Factory*, https://doi.org/10.1007/978-1-4842-8612-8_4

Data Quality

Let's first describe the goals of a data quality ETL job. As a data engineer, you will receive data of all shapes and sizes. It is your responsibility to refine that raw data into data that is ready for business analytics. When working in the cloud with big data, you cannot assume that the condition of the data as it arrives in your data lake is ready for processing. It is very important to establish a set of gated rules that will define what to do with data that does not mean your defined quality standards. To test your incoming data against a set of data quality rules, you can use the Assert transformation. Any row that does not meet those standards will be flagged by ADF. For this scenario, we'll set two rules that define whether the row meets our minimum data quality rules:

1. We are only going to process addresses based in the United States. All other rows will be flagged.

2. The AddressID must be unique. We're going to treat this field as a unique primary key later in the process.

However, before we even check for quality in the data values, we're going to first execute a metadata checker. We have a baseline requirement of these seven fields: AddressID, AddressLine1, AddressLine2, City, StateProvince, CountryRegion, and PostalCode. We're going to ignore the rest of the incoming columns because they are not required for this job. Focusing on just the minimum requirements for an ETL process leads to much more flexible and resilient code. Our rule is going to state that we must have at least each of those fields for the incoming data to pass. Also, since some of our data in other ETL jobs will process the non-US addresses, we will check to ensure that the PostalCode column is a string in order to handle all types of global postal codes later. We'll use the Derived Column transformation with an advanced technique of column patterns, combined with Conditional Split to send only the valid rows to the next step in the pipeline.

Lastly, for the new column called "Full Address", we'll use a Derived Column that will create a new column per row that is based on a combination of AddressLine1, City, StateProvince, and PostalCode. This combined column is needed by another process downstream that will read the Parquet files that we are generating.

Task 1: Start with a New Data Flow

The first thing we're going to do is to build a new data flow from the ADF UI. When you start a new data flow, you need to first connect to your source data by defining a source transformation and provide a meaningful name for your data flow. In Figure 4-1, I called my data flow "Address Quality".

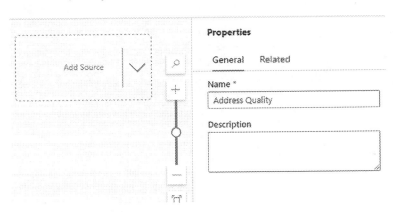

Figure 4-1. *New data flow*

In my data factory, I have a dataset called "Address" that points to my Azure SQL Database with a table from the AdventureWorks schema called "SalesLT.Address" (see Figure 4-2). I chose that dataset as my source in the data flow.

Figure 4-2. *Address dataset*

You can examine the veracity of the data in the source transformation by looking at the Projection tab (Figure 4-3) to view the column metadata and the "Data preview" tab to look at the data samples. Be sure to turn on your debug session in order to import a new projection or to view the data preview (Figure 4-4). Note that when you use a dataset (as opposed to an inline source), the projection will set automatically to the schema in the dataset. However, you can override the schema by using the import projection option from the Projection tab.

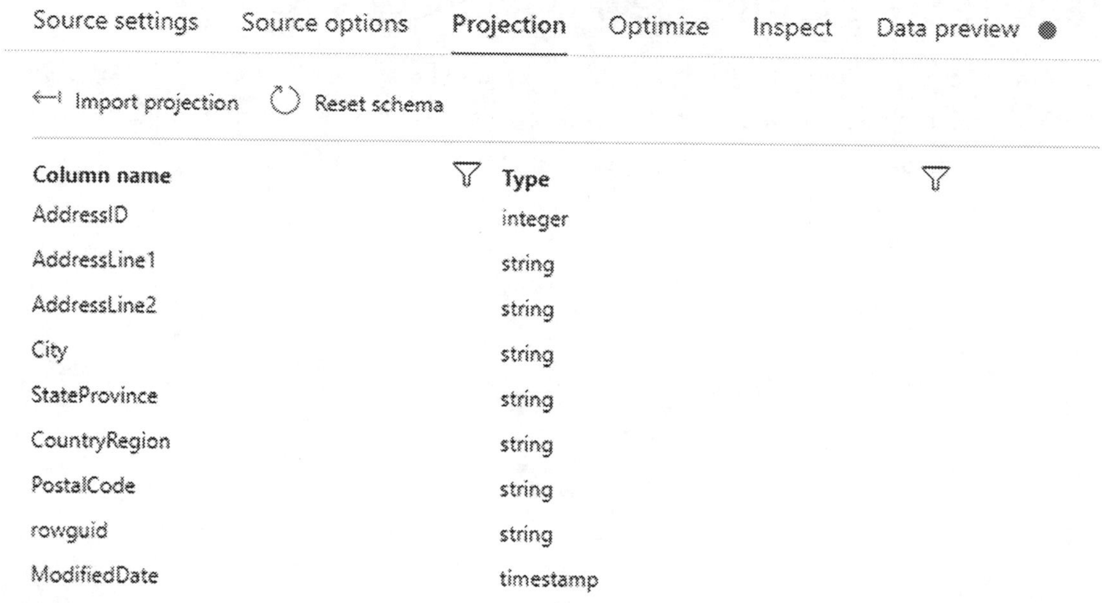

Source settings   Source options   **Projection**   Optimize   Inspect   Data preview ●

⟵ Import projection   ↻ Reset schema

Column name		Type	
AddressID	▽	integer	▽
AddressLine1		string	
AddressLine2		string	
City		string	
StateProvince		string	
CountryRegion		string	
PostalCode		string	
rowguid		string	
ModifiedDate		timestamp	

Figure 4-3. *The source projection*

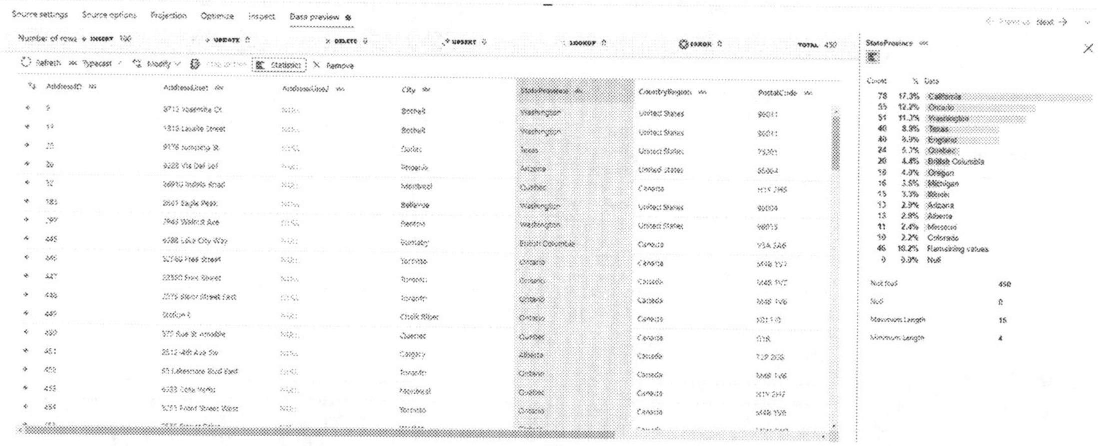

Figure 4-4. *Data preview*

In the data preview screenshot in Figure 4-4, you'll notice that I selected the StateProvince column and then clicked the "Statistics" button. That will open a new pane on the right that shows the data profile for the column selected. In this instance, I'm exploring the shape and patterns of the data in the source transformation and looking at the summary of the distribution of unique values. I noticed that there are no NULLs in this column, which is important for the data to be valid, so let's add a data quality expectation rule to our Assert. Later on, we'll ensure that the StateProvince column is not null and remove any rows that have NULL for this column. This is an example of a natural requirement that emerges from the data engineering process as opposed to a requirement that may emerge from your business users.

Task 2: Metadata Checker

Next, we'll use the Conditional Split to add the metadata checker mentioned previously. We'll split into two streams: Pass and Fail (see Figure 4-5). The Pass stream will allow the data to continue to flow, while the Fail stream will immediately break off by sending the failed rows to a text delimited log file so that we can track which rows did not meet the minimum set of required fields. The formula to determine which rows pass or fail is this:

```
iif(!in(columnNames(),'AddressID'),false(),
    iif(!in(columnNames(),'AddressLine1'),false(),
        iif(!in(columnNames(),'City'),false(),
            iif(!in(columnNames(),'StateProvince'),false(),
                iif(!in(columnNames(),'CountryRegion'),false(),
                    iif(!in(columnNames(),'PostalCode'),false(),true())))))))
```

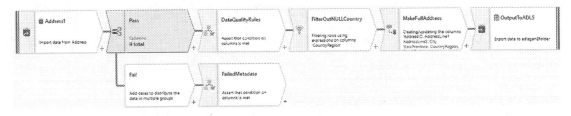

Figure 4-5. *Completed data quality data flow*

Task 3: Add Asserts for Data Validation

Because this scenario is centered on data quality, the Assert transformation in this scenario will do a lot of the heavy lifting here. The first Assert (Figure 4-6) that I'm going to use here is attached to the "Fail" path of the 2nd stream in the previous data flow. I'm using the "Fail data flow" option with an expression that is always true. This way, every time that data flows through this fail path, the data flow will immediately fail and return control back to the pipeline.

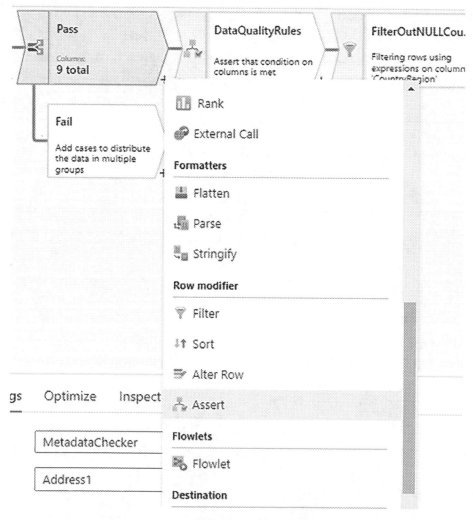

Figure 4-6. *Adding Assert transformation to Conditional Split*

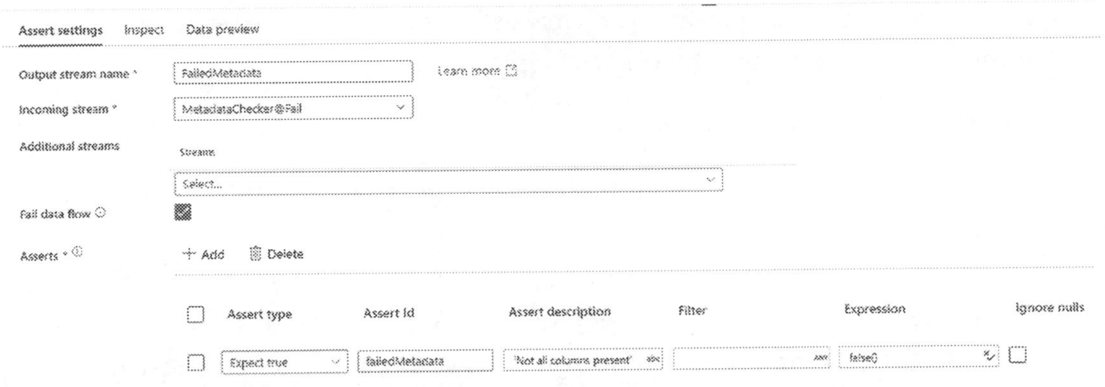

	Assert type	Assert Id	Assert description	Filter	Expression	Ignore nulls
☐	Expect true	failedMetadata	'Not all columns present'		false()	☐

Figure 4-7. *Assert for failed metadata checker*

To add the Assert, select it from the drop-down toolbox after the Conditional Split (Figure 4-6). I've called the assert transformation "FailedMetadata", and this will ensure that the pipeline will always stop when the incoming data does not match my expectations because we do not want to continue processing.

Next, we'll add an Assert transformation directly after the Address source stream, and here, I've renamed it to "DataQualityRules" (see Figure 4-8). The first rule I'll set is for US-only addresses. In Figure 4-8, you can see I've given this first rule an ID of assertUsOnly. The description is a formula that will return the value of the CountryRegion column for each row:

```
CountryRegion + ' is not valid'.
```

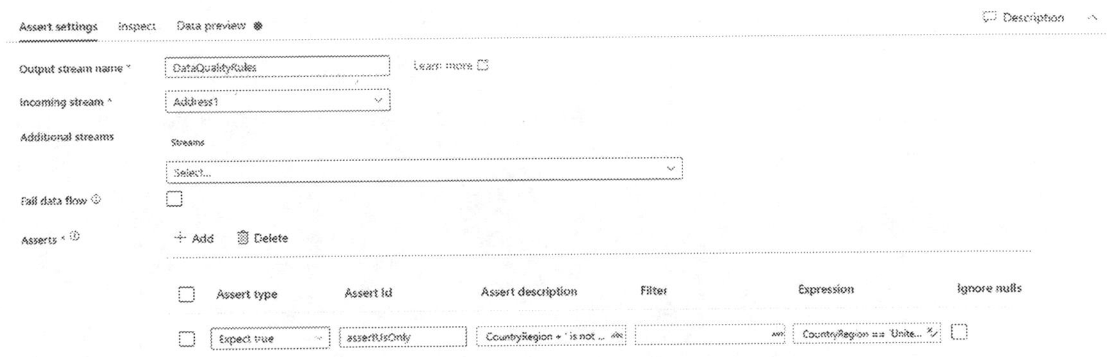

	Assert type	Assert Id	Assert description	Filter	Expression	Ignore nulls
☐	Expect true	assertUsOnly	CountryRegion + ' is not ...		CountryRegion == 'Unite...	☐

Figure 4-8. *assertUsOnly rule*

I'm not going to set a filter so that each row will be evaluated. The expression that is used as the Boolean test for my "Expect true" assertion is

```
CountryRegion == 'United States'.
```

This means that any country other than "United States" will flag this row with an assertUsOnly assertion error.

There is a second rule that I'll add to the Assert using the "Expect unique" assert type. I'll call the assert "addressIdUnique" and set the unique field to AddressID. This will give us the unique primary key property that we set out at the beginning of this chapter. When this assertion fails, I'll use a dynamic description: `"ID of {AddressID} is not unique"`. In ADF, double quotes activate string interpolation. Everything inside of the double quotes will be evaluated as is including the text, functions, and columns when using string interpolation.

Task 4: Filter Out NULLs

Now we need to take out any incoming row that has a NULL value for a CountryRegion value. This is another very common technique in ETL and is a slightly different approach to data cleaning than we took previously where we used Assert to tag rows but still evaluate the row downstream. In data quality jobs, you'll need to make a choice about how to provide clean data to your users. You can remove the bad data, flag it, replace missing values, or change it to valid values. In this case, I'm going to use the Filter transformation to remove rows from this point forward in the data flow where the CountryRegion is NULL. We'll call the transformation "FilterOutNULLCountry". If you look at the data preview statistics for this field (Figure 4-9), you will not see any NULLs. But as a data engineer, it is very important to be defensive and ensure that your jobs are resilient to change.

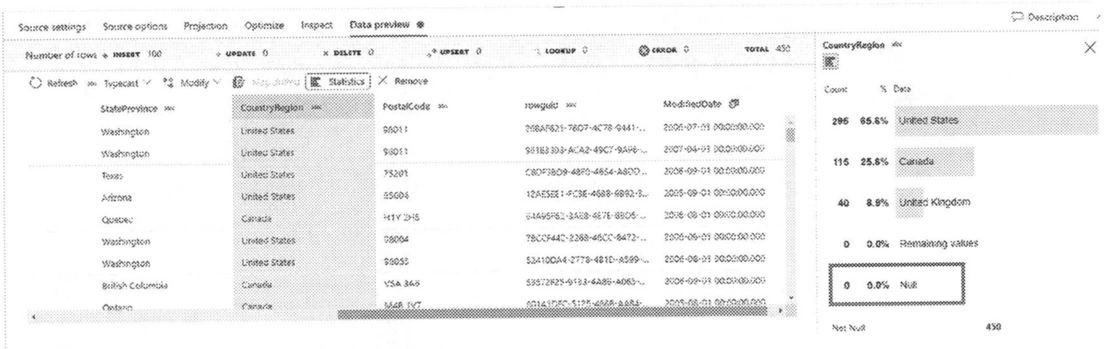

Figure 4-9. *No Nulls found in data preview*

The Filter transformation will protect us from NULLs in this field, which our requirements have deemed as important and require a value. The expression is very simple in this case. We must evaluate to a Boolean so that only rows that match the expression will remain. This expression (resolves to true) for this case will look like this: !isNull(CountryRegion) (Figure 4-10). Notice that in the data preview during debug, the rows will still be visible that are filtered out. The data preview pane will show an X next to the rows that are going to filter out when you execute this data flow from a pipeline.

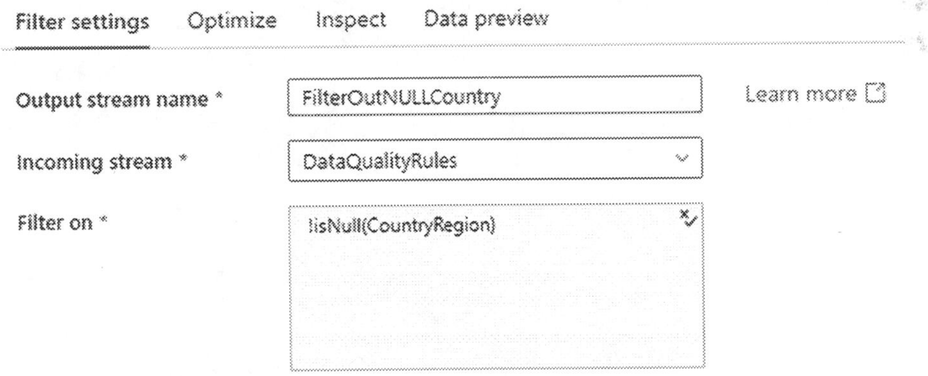

Figure 4-10. *Filter settings for "FilterOutNULLCountry"*

Task 5: Create Full Address Field

Now that we have the full set of required data quality rules addressed, let's address the requirement from the beginning of the chapter that calls for a "full address" field. Since that value is not present in the source data, we'll need to create a new field using a combination of existing columns. To do this, we use the Derived Column transformation. Inside the Derived Column transformation setting panel, I create a new column called "Full Address" and again use string interpolation making this my expression: "{AddressLine1} {City}, {StateProvince} {PostalCode}". Note that I've called the transformation step as "MakeFullAddress" (Figure 4-11).

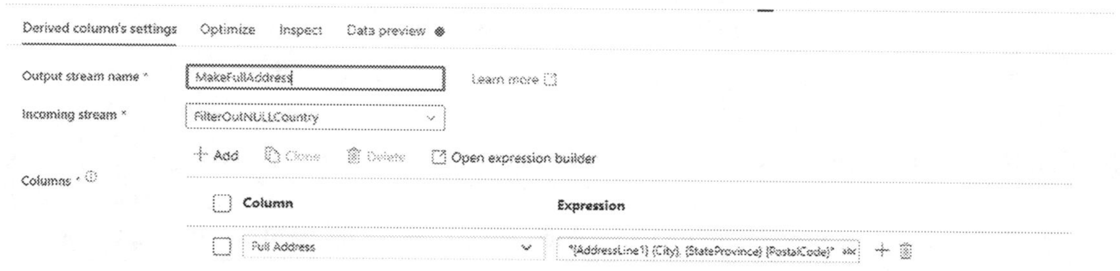

Figure 4-11. *Derived column creates a new column or changes an existing column*

I can use the data preview tab on the Derived Column transformation to test my logic by viewing the results right inside the expression builder. You can see the resulting new calculated column on the left-hand side of the data preview screen in Figure 4-12. Always be sure to check the shape of your data and validate your results using the Inspect tab and data preview tabs on each transformation in your flow.

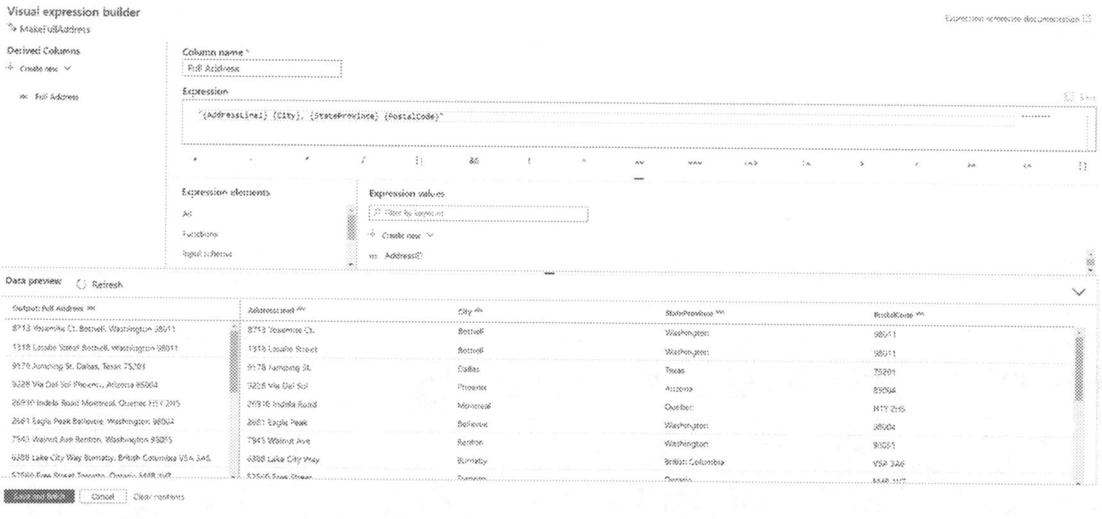

Figure 4-12. *Data preview inside the expression builder*

Final Step: Land the Data As Parquet in the Data Lake

We've completed the tasks in our logic to meet the requirements we set out as our goal. Through the process debugging in the designer, we've validated our approach using data preview. However, this data is currently just sitting in memory as Spark data frames on the serverless cluster that we defined in the Azure Integration Runtime. Every data preview that we have seen here so far in design mode is a snapshot of those in-memory data frames. The final step is to add a sink transformation so that we can store the results as Parquet files in the data lake (Figure 4-13).

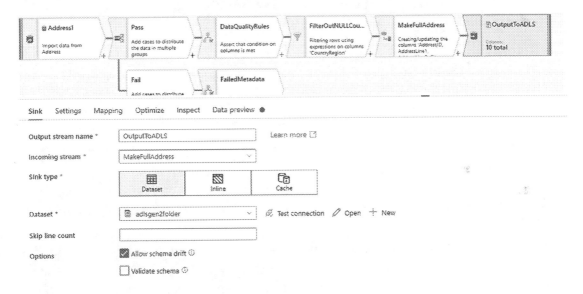

Figure 4-13. *The sink transformation lands the data in the lake*

You'll use the data lake (ADLS Gen2 storage in Azure) very frequently in cloud-first big data ETL projects as your landing zone and staging area. In fact, many projects will maintain historic data as well as hot data in the lake in ADLS and use different compute engines (i.e., Spark, HDI, SQL, etc.) for querying and computation. This is the methodology being used by ADF. You store your data in your data stores, and then the Azure IR spins up the Spark compute as a managed compute environment for data processing for you.

I used an ADLS Gen2 dataset in my sink, which points to a folder in my data lake container. ADF will write the output results to partitioned files in the folder that I specified. In the next chapter, we're going to execute this data flow as a pipeline activity. That is how you will physically serialize your results in a data store at runtime. During design time, data is never written to the sink destination. Even data preview from the sink transformation is just a snapshot of cluster memory. When we dig into the pipeline runtime in the coming chapters, we'll talk about the formatting of the output results. For now, one thing to note here in design mode is that ADF will produce fairly cryptic file names that are based on the Spark distributed processing job IDs (Figure 4-14).

part-00178-829ca3b0-0dbb-4aab-a2c1-6954b0293205-c000.csv	Hot (inferred)
part-00179-829ca3b0-0dbb-4aab-a2c1-6954b0293205-c000.csv	Hot (inferred)
part-00180-829ca3b0-0dbb-4aab-a2c1-6954b0293205-c000.csv	Hot (inferred)
part-00181-829ca3b0-0dbb-4aab-a2c1-6954b0293205-c000.csv	Hot (inferred)
part-00182-829ca3b0-0dbb-4aab-a2c1-6954b0293205-c000.csv	Hot (inferred)
part-00183-829ca3b0-0dbb-4aab-a2c1-6954b0293205-c000.csv	Hot (inferred)
part-00184-829ca3b0-0dbb-4aab-a2c1-6954b0293205-c000.csv	Hot (inferred)
part-00185-829ca3b0-0dbb-4aab-a2c1-6954b0293205-c000.csv	Hot (inferred)

Figure 4-14. *Files resulting from the data flow sink executed from the pipeline*

You can set the partitioning strategy in the sink's optimize tab to adjust the number of partitions being used by the Spark environment. But it is a best practice to leave the partitioning as default so that ADF can expand and shrink the partitions based on the size of the worker nodes that you apply to your job through the Azure IR. If you would like a single output file, you can specify single file output in the sink settings under file name option. But be aware that there is a performance penalty that comes along with this action. This will force ADF to coalesce all of the partitions into a single partition, which can introduce sizable performance lag. Notice that the files being written to the lake in this example are all CSV. I defined that output type in my dataset as delimited text format dataset.

Summary

In this chapter, I introduced the basics of ADF's Mapping Data Flows design surface and the debugging experience. We walked through an example ETL job that focuses on data quality and preparing data for downstream processing by refining incoming data into a more business-ready shape. Now that you have the fundamentals of ETL, ADF, and Mapping Data Flows, let's put those lessons together by building a practical example of an ADF ETL pipeline using data flows in the next chapter.

CHAPTER 5

Common ETL Pipeline Practices in ADF with Mapping Data Flows

In the previous chapter, you learned about Mapping Data Flows in ADF and how to design an ETL pattern for data quality checking, cleaning, and prep. Now that we have a working data flow artifact, we need to execute it from a pipeline. Previously, we were able to peek at samples of the results while designing our logic. This was useful from the perspective of unit testing. The next step in building your ETL solution in ADF will be to test the data flow inside of a pipeline against the full dataset and execute from a debug session. Executing your data flow in the pipeline will write the data out to an ADLS Gen2 data lake folder as Parquet. After verifying the results, we'll build an ETL data pipeline in the ADF pipeline designer that will provide rich workflow capabilities by adding control flow and other activity types in addition to the data flow activity.

Task 1: Create a New Pipeline

Picking up from where we left off in the previous chapter, we're going to take the data flow we just created called "Address Quality" and debug it end to end from a pipeline. To create a new pipeline, you'll go to Factory Resources and click + and then select Pipeline ➤ Pipeline (see Figure 5-1).

© Mark Kromer 2022
M. Kromer, *Mapping Data Flows in Azure Data Factory*, https://doi.org/10.1007/978-1-4842-8612-8_5

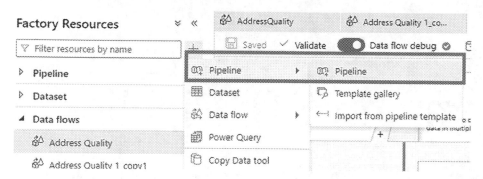

Figure 5-1. *Creating a new pipeline*

On the blank pipeline canvas, find "Address Quality" under "Data flows" (Figure 5-2), drag it onto the canvas, and drop it there (Figure 5-3). Give your pipeline a meaningful name. I chose to call my pipeline "Address Quality Pipeline".

Figure 5-2. *Data flows in the resource explorer*

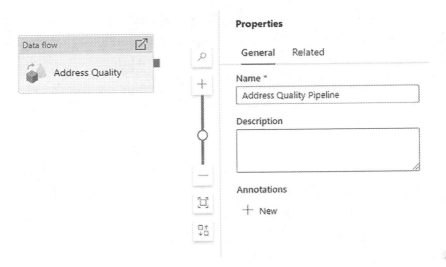

Figure 5-3. *Address quality data flow on the address quality pipeline*

If you have hooked up a Git repo to your factory, you'll be able to save your work. If not, you are essentially connected directly to the live service without the scratch area or branch to work and test in. Later in this book, we'll walk through configuring a connection to Azure DevOps for Git integration. To debug the pipeline, you do not need to publish the factory. You can work with the version of the factory in your browser and in your branch.

Task 2: Debug the Pipeline

Now that you have your data flow in a pipeline, you can begin testing. Make sure that you have the debug session turned on and then click the "Debug" button. Since this pipeline has a data flow activity, you'll need a debug session to be active so that ADF can access a Spark cluster for execution context of your ETL job. The debug button will tell ADF to send the pipeline definition to Logic Apps for workflow orchestration and then take the data flow script payload from your Mapping Data Flow and send that packet to the Spark cluster for execution at scale. Inside the data flow activity settings, you'll see an option for selecting the integration runtime to use for your activity. Just like the debug session, this is default to the auto resolve IR, which is automatically generated at create time of your data factory. In this example, the data is small, so using this default is fine. Notice that you can increase the core count and change the cluster configuration to a memory-optimized option here. More importantly, note that you can choose a different

IR in both the activity settings and the debug session at start time. This allows you to increase the capacity of the cluster being used to execute your debug session and your operationalized pipeline. The Azure IR set in the activity settings will only be used when you execute the pipeline from a trigger or when you select Debug ➤ Use activity runtime (Figure 5-4). You will generally use the default debug session when clicking Debug. But if your pipeline has many data flow activities or data flow jobs that are very large and complex, you may find that the debug with activity IR will provide more Spark compute resources for your debug. You can set the Spark compute via Azure IR in the data flow activity settings (see Figure 5-5).

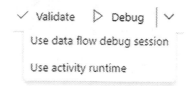

Figure 5-4. *Debug button options in pipeline design mode*

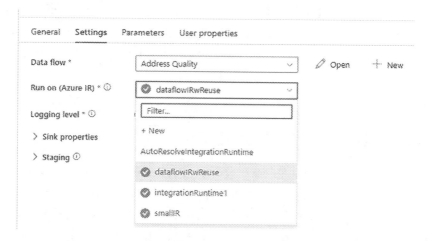

Figure 5-5. *Data flow activity integration runtime options*

There is a trade-off with this approach. If you debug from the activity IR, you may have to warm up the cluster on first debug with that option. The default *debug* option uses the warmed-up cluster from the debug session, whereas run from activity IR uses a separate cluster that has its own life cycle. If you have a TTL set in the Azure IR that you use in the activity, then the next time that you select debug from Azure IR, you may be able to hit a warmed cluster.

Another way to minimize the resource utilization of the Azure IR from your debug session is to leverage the sampling in each of the source transformations. The default is disabled, but if you enable this feature, you can specify a limit for number of rows, which can help to simplify your testing. Just remember to set it back to disabled when you are done before you operationalize the pipeline with a trigger (Figure 5-6).

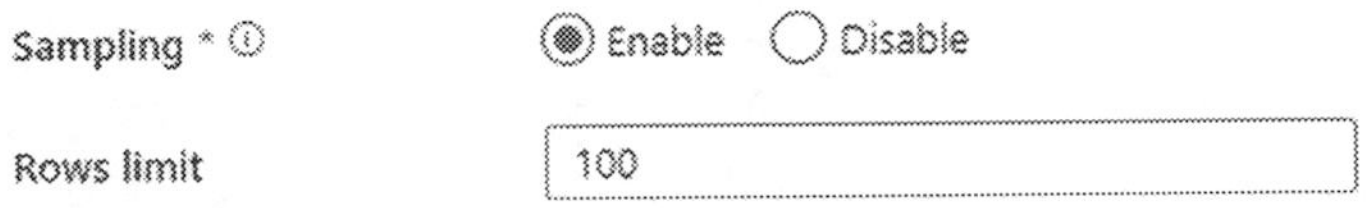

Figure 5-6. *Source sampling*

Task 3: Evaluate Execution Plan

When executing the pipeline with debug, the Output panel on the bottom of your designer will display interactive monitoring of your pipeline process. In the example in this chapter, all we have in the pipeline currently is the data flow activity. At the end of this chapter, we'll add a few more activities to the pipeline for a more realistic operationalized pipeline. But for now, at this point in the process, we just want to continue to unit test the performance and results of the data flow from a pipeline as an atomic unit. The pipeline output will show you the total duration of the pipeline and each activity's status (Figure 5-7).

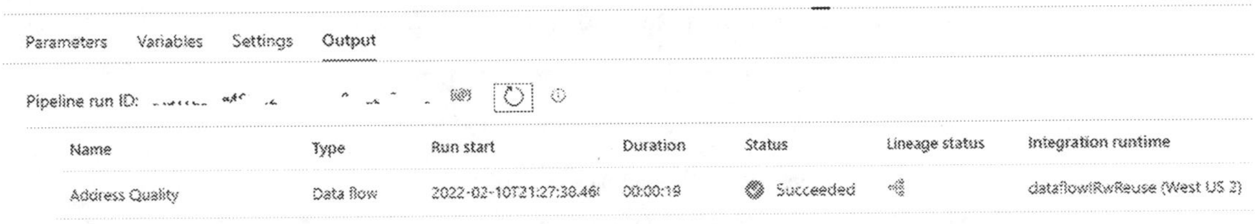

Figure 5-7. *Pipeline interactive monitoring output during debug run*

The lineage view in this pane is connected to Azure Purview so that you can gain holistic insights into your data estate lineage. That is a topic for another book! For now, we'll click on the eyeglasses icon that appears next to the data flow activity in the interactive monitoring pane when we hover over that line. Clicking there will give you a deep introspection view of the execution plan for your data flow. Later in this book, when we monitor unattended pipeline executions, we'll talk more about this view.

For now, since we are testing this single new data flow, let's focus on these five areas in the activity monitoring view for data flow execution. To get to the data flow activity execution plan view, click on the eyeglasses next to the data flow activity (Figure 5-8).

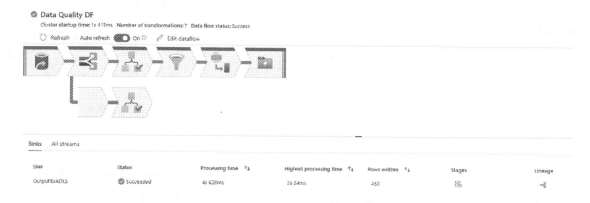

Figure 5-8. Data flow activity monitoring

Let's examine some of the different important components of the data flow activity monitoring details. The following list will detail important data points that you'll use to better understand performance bottlenecks and the path your data took during transformation:

1. Cluster startup time

   This tells you how much time it takes ADF to acquire a Spark compute environment for your data flow. The size of the cluster is determined by the configuration you have set in the Azure Integration Runtime. If you used the debug cluster for this execution, then you will use the warmed-up cluster that is sized based on the Azure IR used for the debug session. If you chose to use the activity IR when you clicked "debug", then the cluster will be configured based on the IR settings in the activity. You should see the total time to be well under one minute here. If it is over one minute, then that means that ADF had to cold-start a new cluster. ADF will only execute one data flow job per cluster.

2. Processing time

This is the total time that ADF spent in Spark execution. The process will start once the executor receives your data flow script from the ADF service, and the clock ends as soon as the processing is complete. What is not accounted for here is the time it takes to serialize the results to disk or database and the time taken by the pipeline for workflow setup and teardown.

3. Rows written

This is important because you can use it as a way to validate your results. The number of rows processed here should be reflective of what you expected to see when your entire dataset was processed. If you had row sampling switched on, you would see a row count here that is indicative of a sampled row count rather than the entire dataset. There is an additional "Rows calculated" value in each of the transformations. Click on the different transformation tiles in your view graph and you can watch the row counts change throughout the life cycle of your data flow.

4. Partitions

So far, throughout this introduction to Mapping Data Flows, and in the example in this chapter, I have kept the partitioning at default "Use current partitioning". Partitioning can be set at each transformation step in the "Optimize" tab. You can view the number of partitions used by ADF in your pipeline execution by clicking on each transformation step. If you have "Use current partitioning" set for transformations, then ADF will not rebalance the partitions throughout the life of your job. However, you can re-partition the data at any step.

In this example, I am using Azure SQL DB as the source with 450 rows. So in this case, ADF will maintain just a single partition. To demonstrate the partition view of the execution in the monitoring view, I want to introduce you to a very important tip when using Azure SQL as a source. Because data flows in ADF execute in Spark, the most optimal configuration for production workloads will be to go into the Optimize tab on the source transformation, click on "Set partitioning", and choose the number of partitions (Figure 5-9).

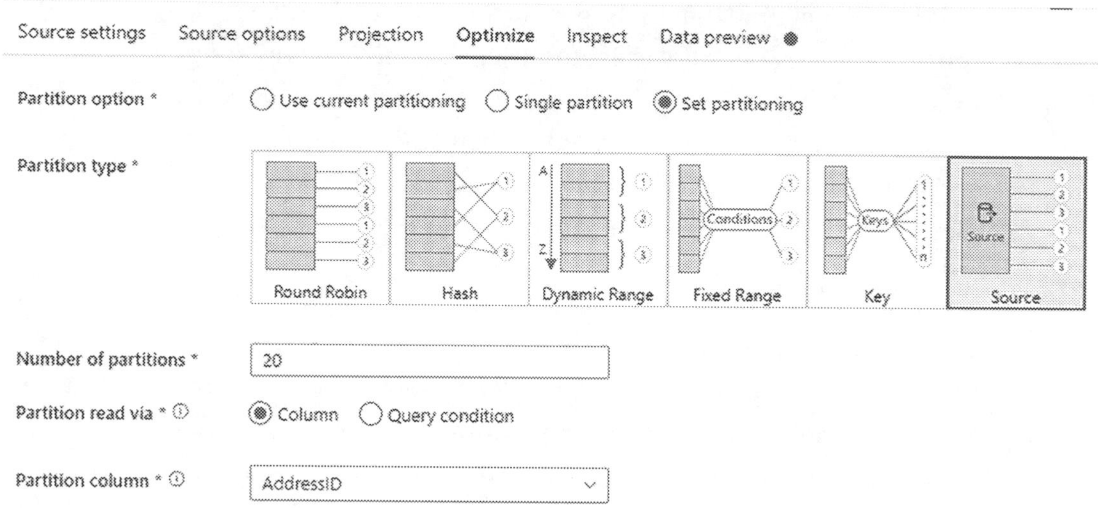

Figure 5-9. *Partition options under "Optimize" in the source transformation*

In this example, I chose 20 because the dataset is small. Also notice that I chose column with high cardinality, "AddressID". That is a good practice, and the number of partitions will depend on your data and the size of the clusters that you have set in your Azure IR. For production workloads, a good rule of thumb is to multiply the number of cores that you have set in your Azure IR worker nodes by 5. So if you have chosen an IR with 32 cores (16 driver + 16 worker), which is a good baseline to use for production workloads, then you would set the number of partitions for the Source partitioning to 16 x 5 = 80 partitions.

5. Pre/Post commands

When you click on the sink transformation to view details, you may see a value for "Pre commands duration" and "Post commands duration" (Figure 5-10). These values will only appear on sinks where ADF had to perf additional operations, or where you specified specific commands to execute as pre- or postprocessing steps. These time values are additive to the total time spent processing your data flow in Spark that is shown on the main activity window "Processing time". The reason for this is that these values are highly variable based on a number of factors: the type of data store being written to, any limits or throttling that may occur on your destination, and any additional properties you may have set in your sink such as shell commands or deleting and moving files post processing. Some examples that will cause higher total execution times that will be reflected here include heavy write volume on your storage containers, which can cause Azure to throttle your connections. Another example is an Azure SQL DB destination that does not have a high-enough capacity set.

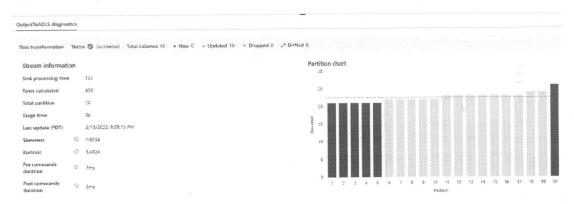

Figure 5-10. *Sink transformation monitoring details*

While we're on the topic of monitoring, I want to point out an important feature in the monitoring view in ADF. Click on the monitoring icon in the left-hand navigation panel and select "Data flow debug" (see Figure 5-11).

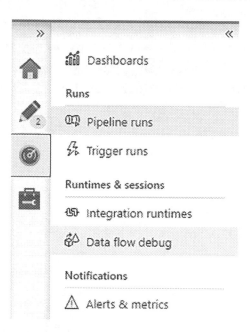

Figure 5-11. *Data flow debug monitoring*

Here, you will be able to see every active debug session currently available in your factory including the user who initiated the session, the compute type, number of cores, and how much time is left in that session. Your debug session timeout (TTL) will reset every time that you perform an action that requires a Spark cluster execution, such as data preview, pipeline debug, or data type detection (Figure 5-12).

Task 4: Evaluate Results

After your debug run has completed, you will want to check the results. When you are previewing the data results in design mode, you can see a sample of the output in the preview pane. However, no data is actually written. Not until you execute from a pipeline will data be serialized to a data store. In this example, we wrote the output as Parquet in the data lake. Parquet is a binary format that requires a data reader, Spark Notebook, or ADF to read. A good way to test the results and view the output is use those mechanisms or create a new dataset in ADF and use the "preview data" dataset feature to validate your results. If you try to open the output Parquet files in Azure Data Explorer on your Windows laptop, you will need to have a Parquet file reader.

Task 5: Prepare Pipeline for Operational Deployment

Before we leave this chapter, let's talk a bit about what an operational pipeline would actually look like as a canonical example rather than just the single data flow activity that we were using for testing. In the following, you'll see how this pipeline that started as a test harness for my data flow eventually becomes a production-ready pipeline (Figure 5-12). This is a very common series of activities in an ETL data pipeline workflow, starting with data acquisition using the Copy activity. In this case, we would utilize the self-hosted IR to access data from an on-premises source and load the data into a staging area in the data lake. A typical pattern would be to land that data in partitioned folders based on day and time so that we can incrementally process data on a schedule. This pipeline would presumably execute on a schedule that fits that data loading pattern, such as daily and hourly. which is achieved by applying a schedule trigger to your pipeline.

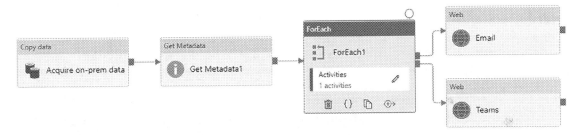

Figure 5-12. *ETL pipeline example*

The next set of pipeline activities will perform control flow and metadata operations against those staging folders and files. The Get Metadata can return the list of files, and then For Each can process each file and folder discovered by providing an iterator over that list. Inside of the For Each container would be the data flow activity that we just completed testing earlier so that the data flow pattern can be parameterized and execute for each file. If you're going to use this pattern with hundreds of files, you will want to set a batch count if you execute data flows in parallel. The preferred mechanism to use in this pattern is sequential in the For Each. The reason for that is each data flow job can only execute one at a time on a cluster. So ADF achieves parallelism in data flow execution by spinning up a cluster per data flow activity when you execute in parallel. That means that you can incur additional spin-up time for each of those clusters and may even eventually exhaust Azure resources resulting in a failed pipeline execution. There is not an implicit additional cost incurred to execute on multiple clusters, but there will be a cold-startup delay incurred while an additional cluster is being formed.

The way to achieve this level of flexibility in your pipeline is through parameterization. We'll talk more about parameters in data flows a bit later in the book. For now, you can assume that each iteration through the For Each loop will send the discovered file name to the data flow as a parameter value. After we've cycled through each file and folder via For Each, processing a data flow for every iteration, we're going to use a web activity to send a notification based on the success or failure return from each of the iterations in the For Each.

Your next steps will be to publish your work through the Git process and assign triggers for unattended execution. Later in this book, we'll walk through an example project with triggers and monitoring from triggered runs as well as how to take the work you've tested in your dev branch, merge that into a main branch, and then publish to the live service in ADF.

Summary

In this chapter, I walked through a series of steps to achieve a common pipeline practice that you should be aware of when building ADF pipelines with data flows. These pipeline practices are a key element in executing your ETL jobs in ADF. I highly recommend that you follow the testing techniques using data preview in the previous chapters together with the pipeline debug methodology described here. Although this chapter did not go into depth on configuration of Git, I also highly recommend connecting your data factory to Git and utilize Git for branching, pull requests, merging, and publishing as part of your life cycle development process. Finally, I demonstrated an example of what a production-ready operationalized ETL pipeline would look like when you add control flow mechanism around the data flow including for each looping, metadata lookups, and copy activity. In the next chapter, we're going to go back into Mapping Data Flows for a deep dive into patterns that you can build and use in your projects including the use of parameters and flowlets to build reusable patterns in your data factory.

CHAPTER 6

Slowly Changing Dimensions

So far in this book, we've covered the basics of ADF's pipelines and Mapping Data Flows. We've walked through common pipeline patterns for cloud-first ETL jobs with ADF and the development and design process. Now let's shift our focus to diving deep into Mapping Data Flows by exploring a few common patterns that you'll use in ADF. In this chapter, we'll talk about the slowly changing dimension scenario. A few of the data flow constructs that we'll use here include derived column, surrogate key, union, alter row, and cached sink transformations. We'll also make use of broadcast optimizations and inline queries.

Building a Slowly Changing Dimension Pattern in Mapping Data Flows

A very common requirement for data engineers building ETL for a data warehouse is handling property changes to dimensional data (business data that describes the measures in your fact table) in a way that maintains the history of those dimension members in your dimension table. We call this pattern a slowly changing dimension type 2 (SCD2). You'll want to become familiar with this requirement because it helps to build a robust data analytics platform that maintains changed rows.

It is not common to update or delete rows inside your data warehouse and treat every data point as an insert. There are exceptions to this rule that include data restatements and archiving old data in batches. But for this scenario, we'll build the pattern using ADF with Mapping Data Flows based on standard SCD type 2 approaches using an active flag and an effective date. A complete end-result example of SCD2 in data flows is shown in Figure 6-1.

© Mark Kromer 2022
M. Kromer, *Mapping Data Flows in Azure Data Factory*, https://doi.org/10.1007/978-1-4842-8612-8_6

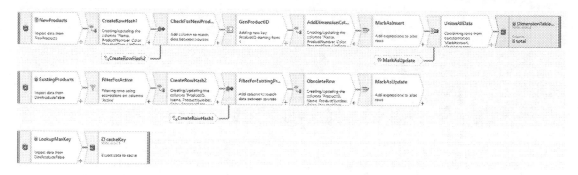

Figure 6-1. *A complete SCD type 2 in Mapping Data Flows*

Data Sources

This pattern will require three sources in your data flow (see Figure 6-2). We are going to model an SCD type 2 for the Products dimension in the free sample SQL Server data warehouse for AdventureWorks (`https://docs.microsoft.com/en-us/sql/samples/ adventureworks-install-configure`). In this example, I am using Azure SQL DB as my source and destination data warehouse and a CSV file for incoming data that is in my ADLS Gen2 data lake. This first example represents an ADF cloud ETL version of a classic SCD type 2 pattern.

Figure 6-2. *Sources required for SCD2*

NewProducts

This source is where you will collect a new set of incoming data that represents a daily
feed of new products to register with your existing product dimension table. The dataset
for this source is a text-delimited dataset pointing to a comma-separated file using an
ADLS Gen2 Linked Service. Here is what the sample data looks like when sampled in an
ADF dataset (Figure 6-3). You can see sample data from the dataset object in ADF using
the preview data button.

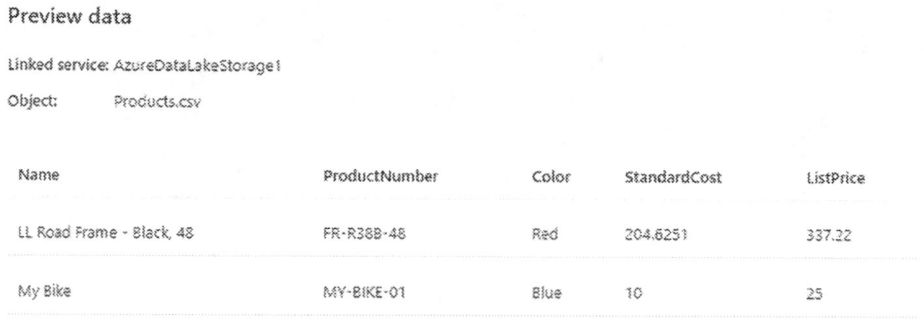

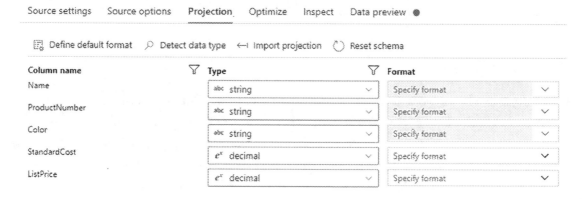

Figure 6-3. *Sample data for new dimension records*

Because this is a text file, there is no inherent data schema associated with the data. However, ADF can infer the data types for you when you have a source that does not contain type information. In the source transformation, click "Detect data type" so that ADF can infer the data types and store the results in your source projection property (Figure 6-4). Note that you must first switch on the data flow debug session using the debug button on the top of your designer window.

Figure 6-4. *Source projection for NewProducts*

As a data engineer, in this scenario, you can expect to receive regular updated data files containing new dimension members from source systems that will generally look similar to this example. We are receiving a text file that contains the product name, product number, color, standard cost, and list price. Product number is the business key that our AdventureWorks sample business systems use for product inventory. However, when you add new rows to a dimension table, you'll want to use the Mapping Data Flow Surrogate Key transformation to add a unique primary key for the row that can be used to relate it back to the fact tables in your dimensional model. The surrogate key is internal only to the data warehouse, so the incoming business data does not have a surrogate key. It is the job of the ETL process to generate unique surrogate keys, while the business keys are used to determine if a new product needs to be added to the dimension table.

ExistingProducts

The ExistingProducts source transformation points to the existing Azure SQL DB table for the Products dimension which I called "DimProductsTable" in my version of the AdventureWorksDW. You can see the table structure in Figure 6-5. Notice that we add the surrogate key in the data warehouse table as ProductID while the business key is ProductNumber. We've also added an EffectiveDate column and an Active column.

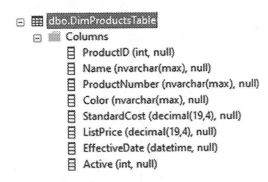

Figure 6-5. *AdventureWorks DimProductsTable*

There are many different methods of building the logic for an SCD2. The end goal is to manage changes in your data warehouse dimension tables by inserting new rows when the properties of an existing dimension member change. In this example, I am doing that by marking the latest version of the row as "Active" using the value of 1. When a new update to the product arrives, I will make Active to be 0 and insert a new row with a new effective date. This way, the business intelligence tools and queries can use a join between fact tables and this product dimension table that looks only for active dimension. In addition, you'll have the date tracking of each dimension row change.

The reason for having a source pointing to the target dimension table here is so that we can compare existing rows with the new data received. We'll need to check each to see if it is an update to an existing product or a new product using the Exists transformation later.

Cached Lookup

The final source is the LookupMaxKey source that uses the same Azure SQL DB dataset as the ExistingProducts source shown earlier. The difference is that we need to use this source as a way to determine the max key value of the surrogate key, stored in the database column "ProductID". To get that value, we'll use the query option on the source transformation using this query where we've aliased the max() SQL function to "maxkey" using a SQL query:

```
select max (ProductID) as maxkey from dbo.DimProductsTable
```

At the end of this short stream, we'll store that value in a cached sink called cacheKey (see Figure 6-6) and use it later to increment the surrogate key as a cached lookup.

Figure 6-6. *Look up the max key value in the dimension table and store it in cache*

Create Cache

To store the max key value in a cache, add a sink transformation and choose "cache" as the type of cache. When creating cached sinks, you can set the key value to match on when using a cached lookup elsewhere in your data flow. However, in this case, since we are only storing the aggregated max value, we do not need to match on any keys. Under Settings, leave the Key Columns empty. Under the Mapping tab, you can choose which columns you wish to return to your cache lookup.

Create Row Hashes

When the ETL job for an SCD2 receives a dimension member that already exists in the target database, we must determine if any property has changed. Only if a change is detected will we update the effective date and active flag. A very effective way to do this is by creating row hashes based on the column properties that you need to track. If you look at the complete data flow from the beginning of this chapter in Figure 6-1, you'll see two Derived Column transformations that create row hashes that are called CreateRowHash1 and CreateRowHash2. In each of those transformations, we are creating a row hash using a set of columns from the incoming new data source and the existing dimension data from the Products table. I'm using the md5 hash function, but you can use other hashing functions in the ADF data transformation expression language:

```
md5(Name,Color,StandardCost,ListPrice)
```

We'll use this cached value a bit later to compare the rows from the different sources to see if any value has changed. We're not actually interested in what the actual value differences are. We just want to use this hashing technique as a way to determine if the product row has changed in any way.

Surrogate Key Generation

In Figure 6-1, there is a Surrogate Key transformation called "GenProductID" that increments the value of ProductID. This value is only used if the product dimension is new or has changed. A bit later in the flow, we will use a Derived Column to add the max product key value from the existing table so that we are certain to always use a unique value.

Check for Existing Dimension Members

In Figure 6-1, you'll see two Exists transformations: CheckForNewProducts and FilterForExistingProducts. In the graph diagram shown in Figure 6-1, you'll see that each of those transformations has a reference node attached to it. ADF draws that on your graph for you as an indicator of which node is associated with your Exists. By setting the right stream (see Figure 6-7), we can tell ADF which transformation stream we want to use for testing for existence of a row value.

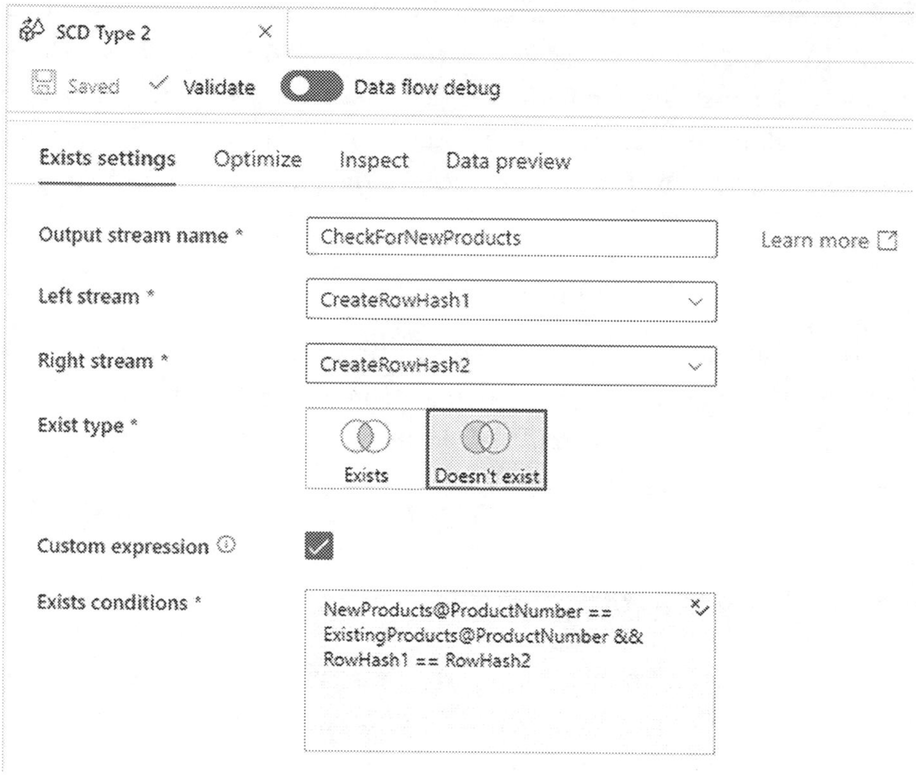

Figure 6-7. *Exists transformation*

The right-hand side here is the CreateRowHash1 transformation from the top stream in our data flow. We are looking into that stream of data to see if this is a new row or an updated row, so we want to eliminate any row coming in from new data that is an exact duplicate of any existing product row in the database table. Since our row hash does not include the business key (ProductNumber), we need to use the custom expression option:

```
NewProducts@ProductNumber == ExistingProducts@ProductNumber && RowHash1 ==
RowHash2 /* Ignore rows that are identical */
```

Also note that I've chosen the "Doesn't exist" option in Figure 6-7. This is because I only want to include rows from the existing table that do *not* have the same product number and row hash.

One final note: There is a message on the top of the Exists UI shown in Figure 6-7 indicating that you should set the broadcast option. It is a good practice to set this because ADF is using Spark for computation and when comparing non-equality against multiple data streams, Spark will perform much better if you instruct the engine to broadcast. What this essentially does is to tell Spark to push the data frame contents of the query to each of the worker nodes, saving shuffling costs. To set this option, click on the Optimize tab in the Exists transformation and pick the smallest side of the data relationship (see Figure 6-8). In my case, the left side is the new rows source, so I chose the left side for broadcast.

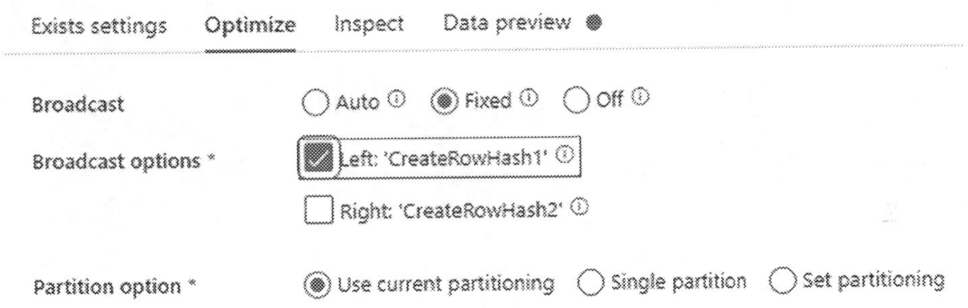

Figure 6-8. Setting broadcast optimization on Exists transformation

Set Dimension Properties

In the completed flow shown in Figure 6-1, the top row represents the stream that processes new products or updated products. The middle row represents existing rows in the database table that need to be updated to being inactive (Active=0). I want to draw attention to two derived column transformations in the flow that set these attributes. You will use derived columns to set row-level properties. The first one we'll look at is in the top row called "AddDimensionColumns". This derived column is only reached in the flow if a new or updated product is found (Figure 6-9).

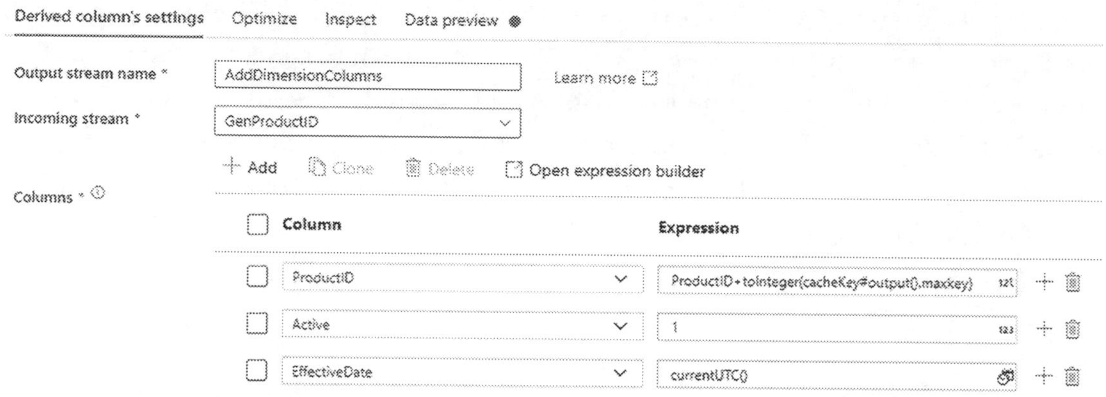

Figure 6-9. *AddDimensionColumns derived column formulas*

There are three attributes that we need to set here that are meant to indicate that this row is to be treated as the new source of truth for this product in the target dimension table:

1. ProductID is the surrogate key value we set earlier. We need to take the "maxkey" value from the SQL query we used in the third source and add it to each surrogate key value to ensure a unique incrementing ProductID. The "maxkey" is stored in the sinked cache we created earlier called "cacheKey". This formula is used to pull that value out of the cache:

    `ProductID+toInteger(cacheKey#output().maxkey)`

2. We will set the value of the Active flag in the database table to 1 here to indicate that this new or updated row is the latest version of the product.

3. EffectiveDate is stamped with `currentUTC()` so that the database table tracks the date in which a product was updated or created.

The second stream in the flow that processes rows that are marked for update uses a single property update in the derived column transformation that is named as "ObsoleteRow". All it has to do is set the Active field to 0. Now that all properties are set for each row type, we can merge these streams and then write the data back to the database.

Bring the Streams Together

The top stream in the data flow in Figure 6-1 and the second stream can be merged in this data flow and at the end of our logic so that we can write results out to a single sink. To do this, I used a Union transformation that I called "UnionAllData". In Figure 6-10, when clicking on data preview for the Union transformation, you can see that we've included one new product (My Bike) and one updated product (ProductID 1013), which has a corresponding update to the former row in the DimProductsTable (ProductID 737).

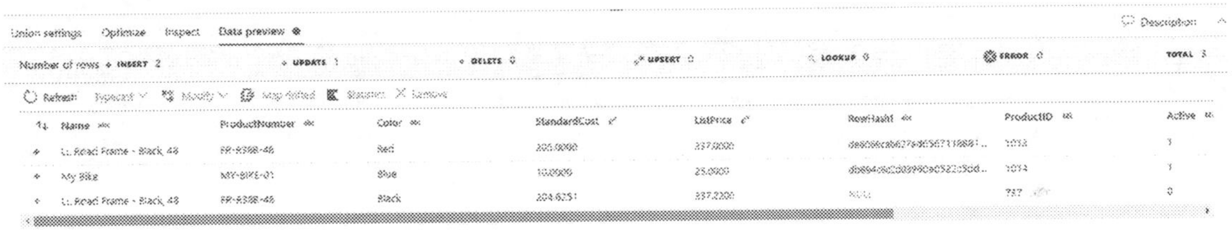

Figure 6-10. *Data preview results from the union of the streams*

Prepare Data for Writing to Database

In order for those updates and inserts to write to the target database table, we use an Alter Row transformation. The Alter Row transformation allows you to tag rows for update, insert, upsert, or delete, based on rules that you define as row policies. In Figure 6-1, that is used twice: "MarkAsInsert" and "MarkAsUpdate". This way, when we union the streams together in the previous section, we'll have the proper row policy in place to handle inserts and updates. The formula for each insert and update policy is simply true() because the data flow that we've designed already separates the inserts from the updates prior to the alter row step.

Because we've merged everything together, we now can use a single database sink to land the data in this dataflow into our target database. The bottom stream is separate (known as a disconnected stream in this graph) and is there solely for the purpose of caching the maximum existing surrogate key in the existing database table.

The sink for this data flow, "DimensionTableSink", takes the consolidated product rows and writes the data to the Azure SQL DB dataset that was used in the database sources: DimProductsTable. In Figure 6-11, you'll see that I've told ADF to expect both inserts and updates from the incoming union transformation. Recall that these row markers were set with the Alter Row transformations.

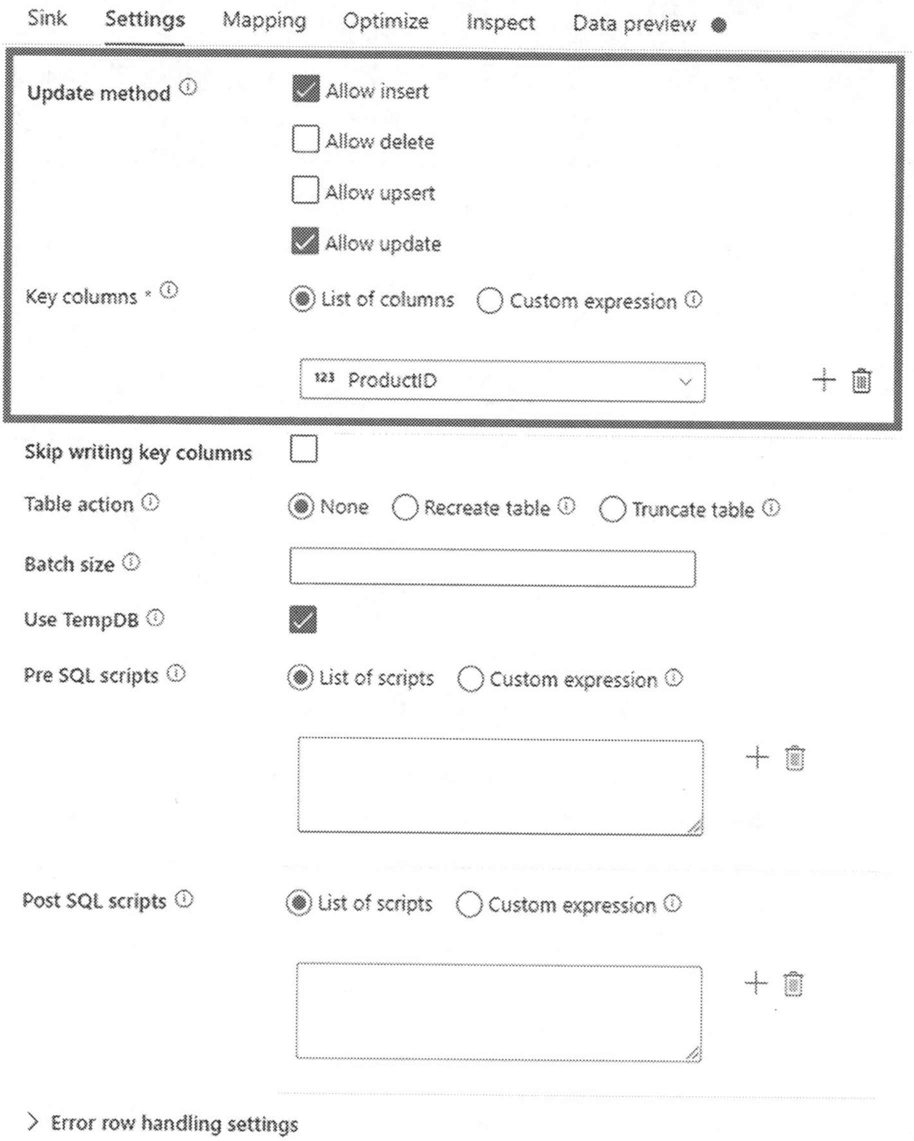

Sink   **Settings**   Mapping   Optimize   Inspect   Data preview ●

Update method ⓘ   ☑ Allow insert

                      ☐ Allow delete

                      ☐ Allow upsert

                      ☑ Allow update

Key columns * ⓘ   ⦿ List of columns   ◯ Custom expression ⓘ

                      [123 ProductID   ⌄]   + 🗑

Skip writing key columns   ☐

Table action ⓘ   ⦿ None   ◯ Recreate table ⓘ   ◯ Truncate table ⓘ

Batch size ⓘ   [   ]

Use TempDB ⓘ   ☑

Pre SQL scripts ⓘ   ⦿ List of scripts   ◯ Custom expression ⓘ

                  [   ]   + 🗑

Post SQL scripts ⓘ   ⦿ List of scripts   ◯ Custom expression ⓘ

                  [   ]   + 🗑

﹥ Error row handling settings

Figure 6-11. *Sink settings for update method*

Also notice in Figure 6-11 that I need to tell ADF what is the primary key so that the update statement can be executed. In this case, ProductID is our primary key.

Figure 6-12 shows the column mapping found in the Mapping panel in the Sink settings panel. This is the list of columns in the target database dimension table, so you'll notice that I removed the row hashes because we do not wish to store them in the target table. They were only used as temporary columns in the data flow for the Exists

transformations. You will use this mapping control in Sink or Select transformations
to set the shape of your data. Optionally, you can set the auto-map feature so that any
column coming into the data flow will land in your target data store. In this example, we
only want to map these specific fields.

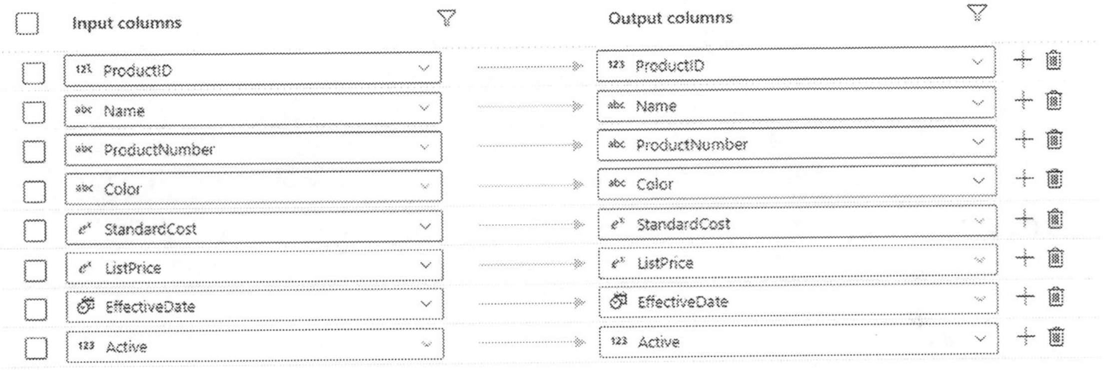

Figure 6-12. *Sink column mapping*

After placing this data flow into an Execute Data Flow activity in my test pipeline, I
ran the pipeline using the debug option. The results are shown in Figure 6-13. ADF wrote
the new My Bike row and updated the LL Road Frame product in the DimProductsTable
dimension table in Azure SQL DB.

	ProductID	Name	ProductNumber	Color	StandardCost	ListPrice	EffectiveDate	Active
1	1014	My Bike	MY-BIKE-01	Blue	10.0000	25.0000	2022-02-27 21:13:23.320	1
2	1013	LL Road Frame - Black, 48	FR-R38B-48	Red	205.0000	337.0000	2022-02-27 21:13:23.320	1
3	1012	Pedals	AA-0000	NULL	NULL	NULL	2022-02-24 09:40:27.540	1
4	1011	Headset Ball Bearings	BE-2908	NULL	NULL	NULL	2022-02-24 09:40:27.540	1
5	1010	Blade	BL-2036	NULL	NULL	NULL	2022-02-24 09:40:27.540	1
6	1009	BB Ball Bearing	BE-2349	NULL	NULL	NULL	2022-02-24 09:40:27.540	1
7	1008	Bike	AR-5381	blue	0.0000	0.0000	2022-02-24 09:40:27.540	1
8	1007	My Nice Bike	ABC123	Red	10.0000	20.0000	2022-02-24 09:40:27.540	1
9	999	Road-750 Black, 52	BK-R19B-52	Red	343.6496	539.9900	2022-02-24 09:40:27.540	1
10	998	Road-750 Black, 48	BK-R19B-48	Black	343.6496	539.9900	2022-02-24 09:40:27.540	1

Figure 6-13. *Results of data in target database table after executing the pipeline*

A final note on the configuration for the data flow that is set in the settings tab
on your data flow. Click on the open whitespace on your data flow design to view the
Custom Sink Ordering (Figure 6-14). Since we are using a cached sink for the max key
value, ADF automatically sets the sink order for you with the cached sink as the first sink
in the write order. When using a cached sink, you must set the cached sink to execute

first before any of the other sinks can serialize your results to a data store. You can manually set the order of your sinks from this screen.

Figure 6-14. *Data flow settings for sink ordering*

Summary

In this chapter, we used the features in ADF's Mapping Data Flows that we talked about in the earlier chapters to build a common pattern called a slowly changing dimension. This is a pattern that you'll use very often when loading analytical database schemas in your ETL projects. In the next chapter, we'll continue this deep dive into building data flows with another common pattern: data deduplication.

CHAPTER 7

Data Deduplication

In the previous chapter, we went into depth on our first data flow pattern in this book, walking through the common slowly changing dimensions pattern. In this chapter, we'll continue the deep-dive exploration with another data flow pattern. This time we'll cover data deduplication.

The Need for Data Deduplication

Part of the role of data engineering and ETL jobs is to ensure that the data being processed for business use is clean and contains a single source of truth. Deduping data is extremely important and a very common pattern that you can reuse in many ADF pipelines.

In the cloud big data world and in data lakes in general, you are going to very often find data with duplicates or possible duplicates that will require row scoring and fuzzy matching. For our data deduplication sample, we're going to split this problem into two subpatterns:

- For the first pattern, we'll take advantage of ADF's schema drift feature to implement a very simple row hashing and exact matching technique to remove duplicate rows all together for what I'll term as a "distinct rows" pattern (Figure 7-1).

- In the second pattern, we'll use built-in ADF algorithms found in the data flow transformation expression language to perform fuzzy matching. We'll also score each row with a likely match to determine which rows are likely duplicates and then produce separate output files of rows that did not have any apparent matches and rows that met the threshold for possible duplication.

© Mark Kromer 2022
M. Kromer, *Mapping Data Flows in Azure Data Factory*, https://doi.org/10.1007/978-1-4842-8612-8_7

The second pattern is much more complicated than the first with a lot of logic that would be useful in other data flows. So we'll take the logic from the fuzzy dedupe data flow and make it into a reusable component using the ADF "Flowlets" feature.

Type 1: Distinct Rows

This first style of data deduplication is very simple and straightforward. The basic concept is that we are going to generate a unique fingerprint of each row by hashing the column values in the source data using the derived column transformation in Figure 7-1 called "MakeRowHash".

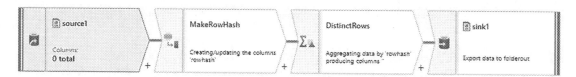

Figure 7-1. *Distinct rows data flow*

We can make this pattern fully dynamic in a few steps listed as follows. Combining these three techniques of schema drift, late schema binding, and column pattern transformations can make your data flow very flexible.

1. Make sure that "Allow schema drift" is set on in the Source transformation. Schema drift handling is on by default in ADF (Figure 7-3). This tells ADF to allow any new columns from the source to flow through your streams even if the column is not defined in the source projection. You can visually detect which columns are drifted via schema drift from the data preview tab (Figure 7-2). The column header will include a "drift" icon for schema drift columns. You can also programmatically determine schema drift columns using the `columnNames('',true())` function, which will return only column names that are schema drift columns.

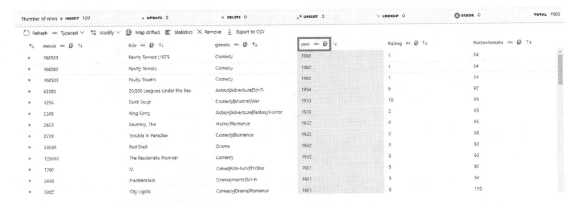

Figure 7-2. *Schema drift indicated in data preview with drift icon*

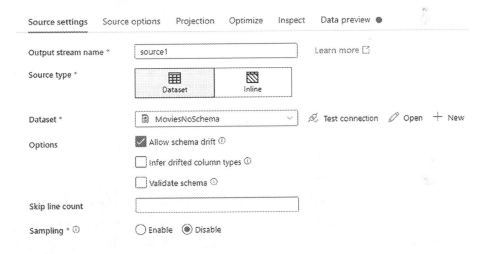

Figure 7-3. *Allow schema drift default setting in ADF Mapping Data Flow source*

2. In the source dataset schema and the source data flow
    transformation, do not define a schema. The projection tab in
    the source should be empty. In ADF, we call this "late schema
    binding." Establishing a known schema early in the ETL process
    through a dataset schema and a source projection is "early
    binding." Early column binding is useful when you need to
    validate a well-known schema from your source data and wish
    to access columns directly by name in your transformation
    expressions. But in the big data cloud analytics world, late binding
    is very common because the nature of data in the lake can be

very indeterminate and unknown. Late binding combined with schema drift handling can make your data flows much more resilient to change.

3. When working with late binding in mapping data flows, you will need to use pattern techniques to transform individual fields since the metadata will not be known by ADF at design time because your flow is not binding the schema until later. In this data flow, I used the column pattern technique to aggregate rows using the row hash created in the derived column "MakeRowHash". When you look at the Inspect tab of data flows that utilize late schema binding without a projection in the source transformation, you will not see any columns unless you manually create them using a derived column or other column-generating transformation.

To make row hashing generic for all columns, regardless of the column names defined in each row, use this formula to create a new column called "rowhash":

```
sha2(256,columns())
```

That tells ADF to create a row hash for every value in every column per row, without needing to bind to the names of each column.

The final step before sinking the data into the data lake is the "DistinctRows" transformation. This is an aggregate transformation where we will use the group by feature of aggregation to remove duplicate hashes. Set the Group By property to the "rowhash" column that was generated earlier using the generic derived column formula. In Figure 7-4, I chose to create a new column pattern in the aggregate using the set of aggregation rules shown in Figure 7-5.

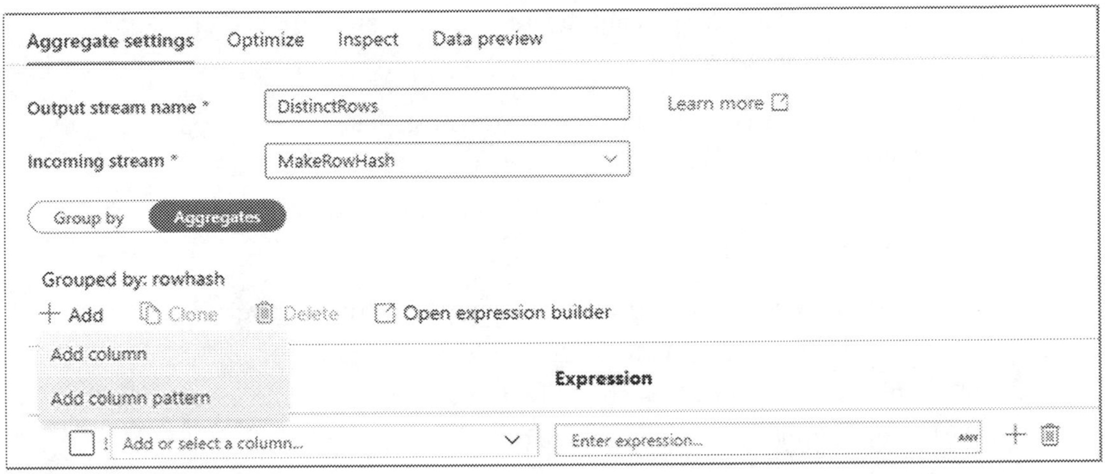

Figure 7-4. *You can choose to add a new column or a new column pattern in the aggregate transformation*

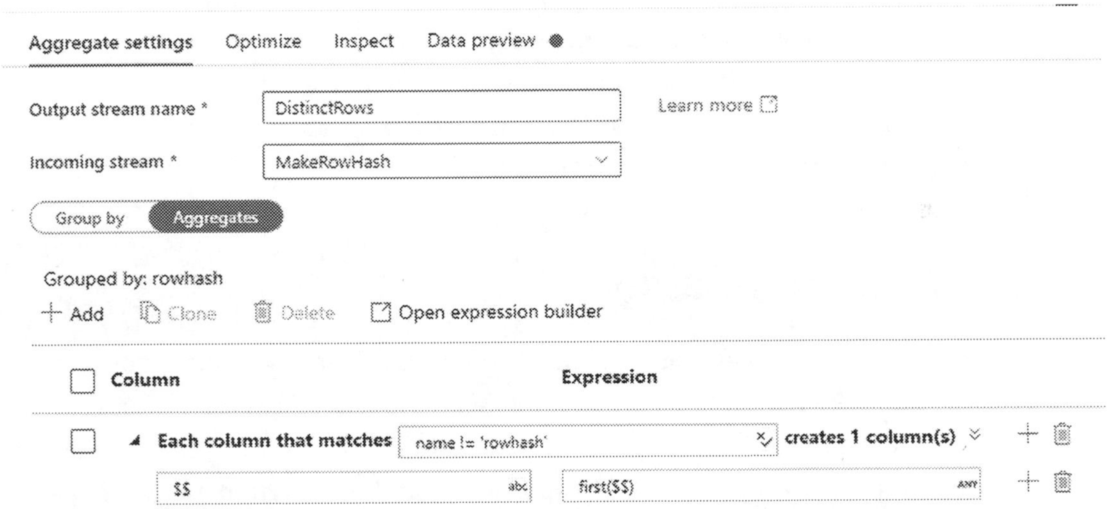

Figure 7-5. *Aggregate transformation using column pattern matching*

Follow these steps to configure an aggregate transformation that can remove duplicates in a single step:

1. Find every column that is not named "rowhash" using `name !='rowhash'`. This removes the current column that I am actively grouping on in the group by clause so that the column is not duplicated in the output.

2. Use the $$ syntax to define the current column name for every discovered column that matches the pattern. You can think of $$ in mapping data flows as equivalent to `this` context that is common in programming language concepts.

3. The third property defines the value to set for every column. Since I am using Aggregate for my distinct rows technique, I have to use an aggregate function here. I chose `first($$)`, which instructs ADF to pick the first match when duplicates are found and drop any other matched rows. You can optionally choose `last($$)` here if your logic works better using the last matched duplicate row. When eliminating exact row duplicates, it does not typically matter which row you decide to keep.

Type 2: Fuzzy Matching

Now let's dive into how to use fuzzy matching techniques and row scoring to determine possible duplicate rows in your data. This sample serves as a good example of how to add fuzzy matching and scoring to your scenarios. Rather than describe the complete end-to-end flow shown in Figure 7-6, I'll instead focus on the important areas of logic that you can reuse. The complete sample is available in ADF under the data flows section of pipeline templates. You can create the pipeline sample with this data flow by going into your factory and selecting New pipeline > from template. Let's walk through the important logical constructs that I used to create this pattern. These techniques will be important for you as you apply these patterns in your own data flows in your factory. An important difference between the goal of this pattern and the first distinct rows sample from this chapter is that rather than perform a fingerprint exact match review of the data, this data flow will instead look for the possibility of matches.

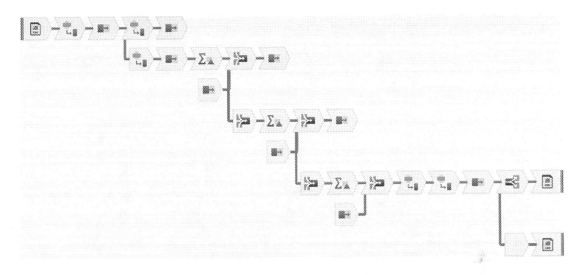

Figure 7-6. *Complete fuzzy matching deduplication data flow in ADF*

This sample is based on four columns that define an employee using just four attributes: phone number, zip code, full customer name, and employee ID (sample data available here). The use case is that you could use this data flow when processing data for your human resources data warehouse.

Let's start by looking at the top line of the data flow (Figure 7-7). We are going to turn this into a reusable pattern at the end of this chapter by converting it into a "Flowlet", so I'll skip over the initial source and derived column ("CreateFullName") transformations. The source data is essentially irrelevant because we're going to map to a semantic model in the "MapNames" Select transformation. The CreateFullName is simply a derived column that concatenates first name with last name to create the full name that is needed by this data flow in order to use Soundex name matching.

Figure 7-7. *Top stream in the data flow*

In the "MapNames" Select transformation, I am building a semantic model that maps incoming data sources to column names that I use as the logical metadata through the remainder of the data flow. In this sample, I know the left-side incoming source columns, so simply direct mapping using fixed mapping in the Select works well (Figure 7-8).

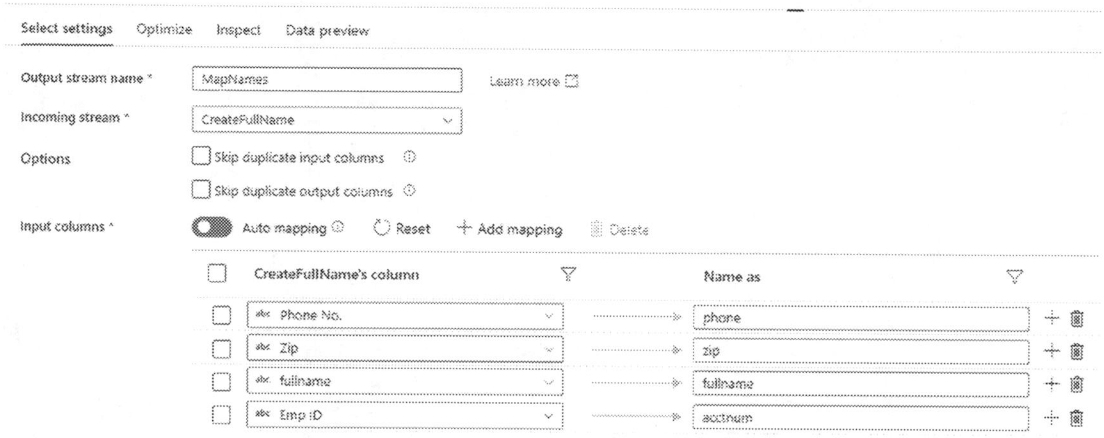

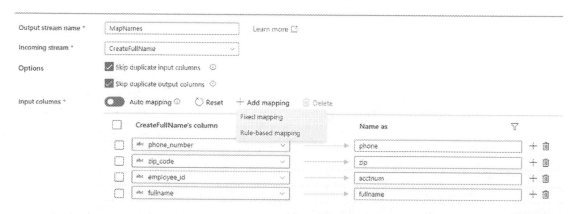

Figure 7-8. *Create a semantic model by mapping columns*

Column Pattern Matching

Here is how to make this a more flexible generic pattern that can work for any incoming data as long as the incoming data contains phone, zip, full name, and ID. If you use the rule-based option in the Select transformation (see Figures 7-9 and 7-10), you can look for patterns in the incoming column names and then match them to your canonical model on the right-hand side. The `instr()` function looks for existence of a string inside another string and provides the starting index when found. If the return is greater than 0, then we know that field is a match. Using this method, we will now have a semantic model to use for the remainder of the transformation allowing us to eventually turn this into a reusable Flowlet later in the chapter.

Figure 7-9. *Choose rule-based mapping as the "Add mapping" type in the Select transformation*

	CreateFullName's column			Name as		
☐	instr (lower(name),'phone') > 0	X	» ·····››	'phone'	abc	✛ 🗑 ⊗
☐	instr (lower(name),'zip') > 0	X	» ·····››	'zip'	abc	✛ 🗑 ⊗
☐	instr (lower(name),'fullname') > 0	X	» ·····››	'fullname'	abc	✛ 🗑 ⊗
☐	instr (lower(name),'id') > 0	X	» ·····››	'acctnum'	abc	✛ 🗑 ⊗

Figure 7-10. *Rule-based column mapping in the Select transformation*

When using this column pattern matching technique, the incoming and outgoing metadata will display your results from the Inspect tab. In the ADF dedupe sample employee data, you'll notice that the source data has many more fields (Figure 7-11). After applying these matching patterns to our model, the remaining columns in the stream will only be those four columns that now make up our projection as shown when clicking the Output button on the Inspect tab of the Select transformation (Figure 7-12). What we have essentially accomplished through these steps is to define our projections manually rather than through the source Projection option.

Select settings   Optimize   Inspect   Data preview ⚙

Schema   Input   Output

Number of columns **Total** 38

Order ↑↓	Column ↑↓	Type ↑↓
1	Emp ID	abc string
2	Name Prefix	abc string
3	First Name	abc string
4	Middle Initial	abc string
5	Last Name	abc string
6	Gender	abc string
7	E Mail	abc string
8	Father's Name	abc string
9	Mother's Name	abc string
10	Mother's Maiden Name	abc string
11	Date of Birth	abc string
12	Time of Birth	abc string
13	Age in Yrs.	1,2 double
14	Weight in Kgs.	abc string
15	Date of Joining	abc string
16	Quarter of Joining	abc string
17	Half of Joining	abc string
18	Year of Joining	abc string

Figure 7-11. *Employee sample data from the previous sample file example*

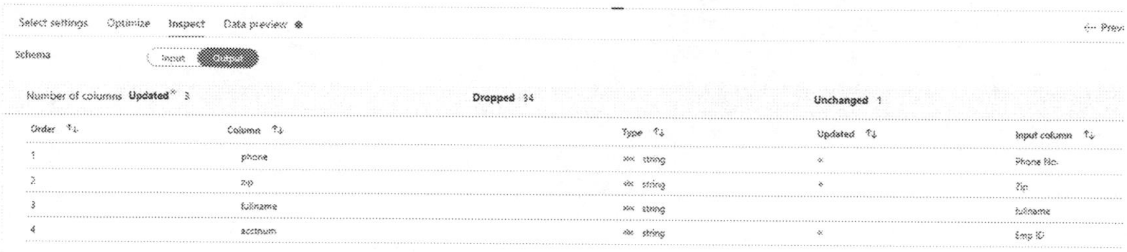

Figure 7-12. *Output of Inspect shows matched metadata*

Self-Join

A very important concept utilized in this sample data flow is self-joins (Figure 7-13). In mapping data flows, this pattern is very common when using aggregate transformations. Aggregates, by nature, reduce columns and reduce rows. So if you wish to perform an inline aggregation as is done multiple times in this sample, you will need to first branch off the primary stream using New Branch. The new branch will duplicate the current stream and provides you with a very convenient mechanism to process the same data in different ways in separate streams inside your data flow. After performing your aggregation, you'll rejoin the aggregated data back with the original set of rows and columns using a key column. Aggregation is used in this flow as a way to sum up the number of matches of zip, phone, and full name. Notice that when I branched for each aggregation, I utilized the Select transformation to rename the previous stream as "soundexBranch", "phoneBranch", and "zipBranch". This is a good practice so that it is easy to define and recognize the different paths and streams that were branched in your graph, making your transformation formulas easier to read and understand as you add more branching.

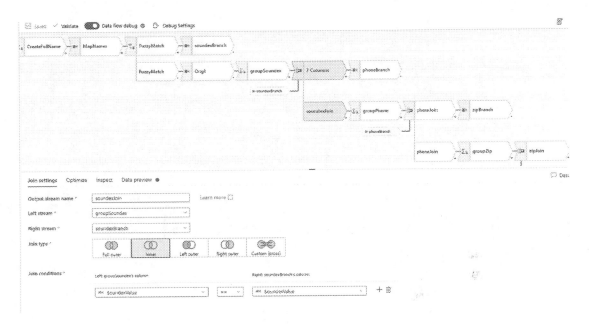

Figure 7-13. *Self-join pattern*

The fuzzy matching used in the sample is the sounds-like phonetics matching algorithm used in the built-in soundex() ADF function applied to the FullName column. This is applied to a new column named "SoundexValue" using the derived column called "FuzzyMatch".

In order to have the full set of rows and columns for the self-join, add a New Branch to the FuzzyMatch Derived Column. Now you should see a second stream added below it also called "FuzzyMatch". Add a Select transformation to that new branch and call it "Orig1" to match the previous diagram. I'm calling it that because it contains all of the original columns and rows. Next, add a Select transformation to the FuzzyMatch derived column transformation. In my example, I called it "soundexBranch" (Figure 7-14) to label it for the self-join later.

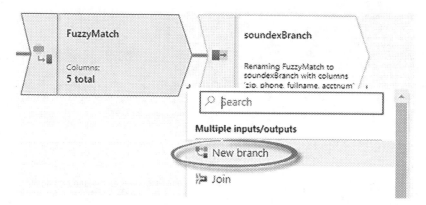

Figure 7-14. *Adding a New branch will duplicate the current stream*

Now add the Aggregate transformation called "groupSoundex". Here, we'll group by SoundexValue, thereby reducing rows and summing the total number of matched per name value. We can use the aggregate for deduplication by grouping rows with the same SoundexValue. Set the Group by column to SoundexValue (Figure 7-15). The expression will simply be sum(1) and a new column called "soundexmatch" (Figure 7-16). This will give you a count of every matched SoundexValue row.

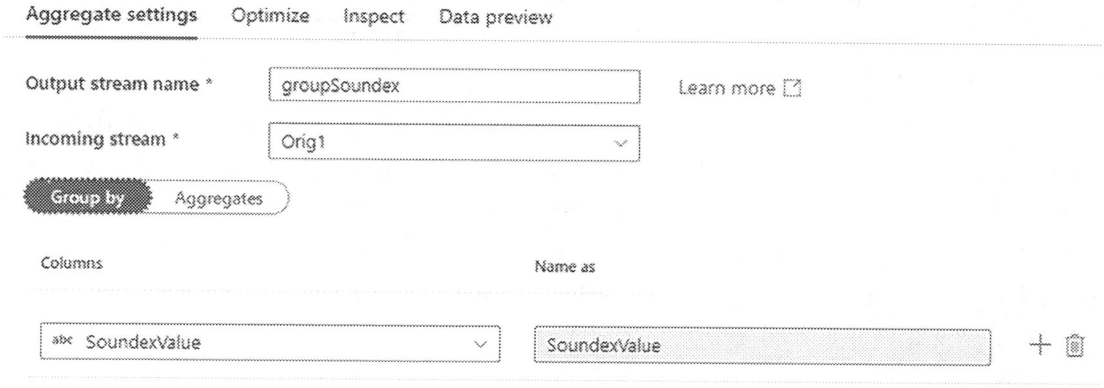

Aggregate settings   Optimize   Inspect   Data preview

Output stream name *	groupSoundex	Learn more ☐
Incoming stream *	Orig1	

Group by   Aggregates

Columns	Name as	
abc SoundexValue	SoundexValue	+ 🗑

Figure 7-15. *The aggregate transformation group by is used in this case to group by duplicate rows based on the SoundexValue column and then count the number of matches*

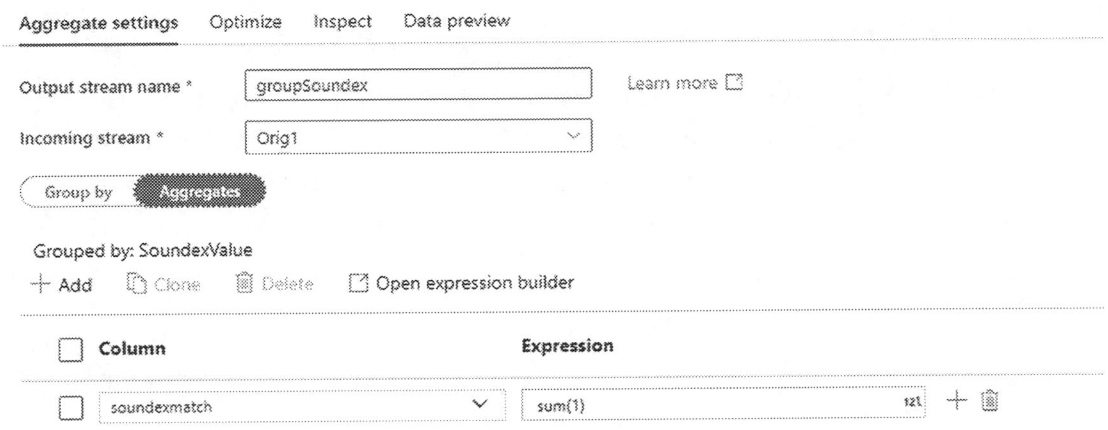

Aggregate settings   Optimize   Inspect   Data preview

Output stream name *   [groupSoundex]   Learn more ☐

Incoming stream *   [Orig1   ⌄]

(Group by   **Aggregates**)

Grouped by: SoundexValue

╋ Add   ☐ Clone   🗑 Delete   ☐ Open expression builder

☐	Column	Expression
☐	[soundexmatch ⌄]	[sum(1) 121] ╋ 🗑

Figure 7-16. *The aggregate function for groupSoundex is simply sum(1) to add all matched rows for a total count*

You should now have one branch that contains just the aggregated/reduced rows and columns from the aggregation "groupSoundex" and one branch that contains all of the original data (soundexBranch from Figure 7-14). This will allow you to perform the self-join using the Join transformation. Add a Join transformation to the Orig1 branch, and for the right-hand stream, select "soundexBranch". You will perform an inner join on the SoundexValue, and that will bring your full stream of data back together with the new aggregated sum column "soundexmatch" and includes all of the stream's metadata (Figure 7-17)

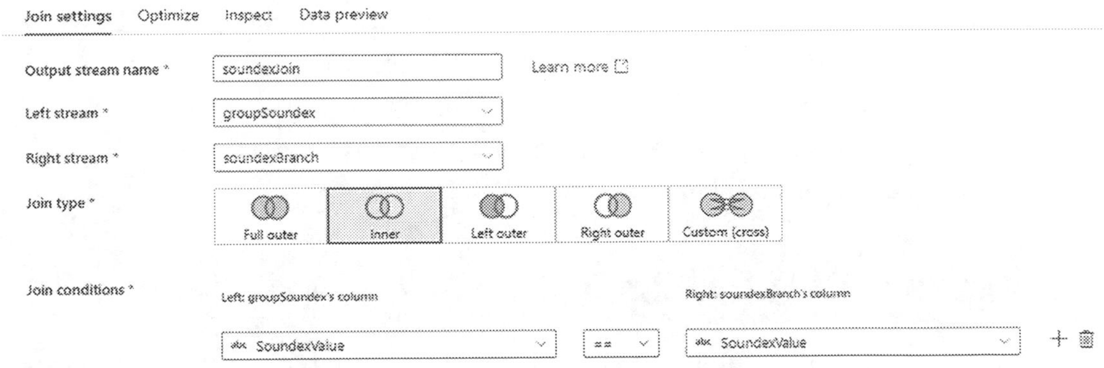

Join settings   Optimize   Inspect   Data preview

Output stream name *   [soundexJoin   ]   Learn more ☐

Left stream *   [groupSoundex   ⌄]

Right stream *   [soundexBranch   ⌄]

Join type *

⌾⌾	⌾⌾	⌾⌾	⌾⌾	⋈
Full outer	Inner	Left outer	Right outer	Custom (cross)

Join conditions *

Left: groupSoundex's column   Right: soundexBranch's column

[abc SoundexValue   ⌄] [== ⌄] [abc SoundexValue   ⌄] ╋ 🗑

Figure 7-17. *Join on the SoundexValue to bring back the streams as a self-join*

Match Scoring

To build a scoring routine, let's navigate down the Mapping Data Flow graph to the "groupPhone" aggregate for our first example (Figure 7-18). If you are having trouble navigating the graph to find a transformation, use the search button on the right-hand portion of the graph display and search for the name "groupPhone".

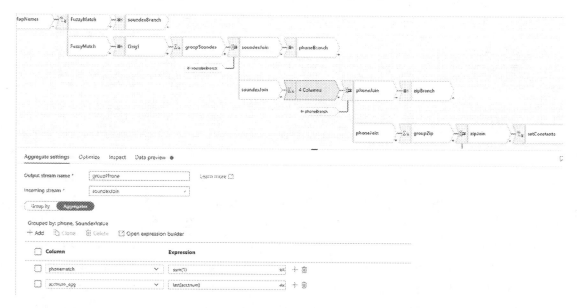

Figure 7-18. *Aggregate transformation used for deduping*

This transformation is an aggregation, and the group by uses two properties: phone and SoundexValue. This way, we can both count the number of occurrences of this match using sum(1) and eliminate duplicates of the ID field using last(acctnum). You should already be familiar with that dedupe technique from the first example in this chapter. The reason to sum up the number of matches is to use later in scoring. In this data flow, we'll sum up the total matches found for phone and zip.

Scoring Your Data for Duplication Evaluation

The nature of employee matching data is that while phone numbers and zip codes may be identical, it is still possible that the employee record is not a perfect match. By using "acctnum" as a group by property in the aggregations, we eliminate exact primary key matches. But for the name phonetic sound, zip code, and phone number fields, we'll devise a simple mathematical model to apply a score using these rules:

1. Apply 50 points for names that sound alike. This accounts for data quality issues such as typos or misspelling of names.

2. Apply 25 points for exact zip code matches. A zip code match on its own should be weighted low because it does not indicate a match but is important as a matching criterion when combined with other employee properties.

3. Twenty-five points for a phone match. Phone numbers can still be identical for different employees.

Notice in Figure 7-19 for the "setConstants" derived column, we also set a Boolean for each property to see if there were matches found for each category by applying an iif() rule that sets each Boolean to true if there was more than one entry found in the data for each category.

Derived column's settings	Optimize	Inspect	Data preview

| Output stream name * | setConstants | | Learn more |
| Incoming stream * | zipJoin | | |

+ Add   Clone   Delete   Open expression builder

Columns *

	Column		Expression	
☐	soundexweight	⌄	50	123
☐	zipweight	⌄	25	123
☐	phoneweight	⌄	25	123
☐	soundexbool	⌄	iif (soundexmatch > 1, 1, 0)	123
☐	zipbool	⌄	iif (zipcount > 1, 1, 0)	123
☐	phonebool	⌄	iif (phonematch > 1, 1, 0)	123

Figure 7-19. *A derived column transformation called "setConstants" is setting values that we'll use to update in the target table*

Now that the constants have been set, let's calculate our formula in the next derived column called "matchScore":

```
(soundexbool * 50) + (zipbool * 25) + (phonebool * 25)
```

That formula gives our final score that will be evaluated for matching likelihood next, setting a new column to that formula that is called "matchscore".

Next, we'll use the Conditional Split transformation shown in Figure 7-20 to evaluate each row for a possible match using the "matchscore" calculation shown earlier. The conditional split will split your data flow based on different values. In this case, I've chosen 50 as the cutoff value for considering a row as a possible match. When the value is over 50, we send the output to the "sinkDupes" sink to write the rows as duplicates. Then, we'll send all other values to the "NotDupe" path and write those rows to the folder that contains each unique employee.

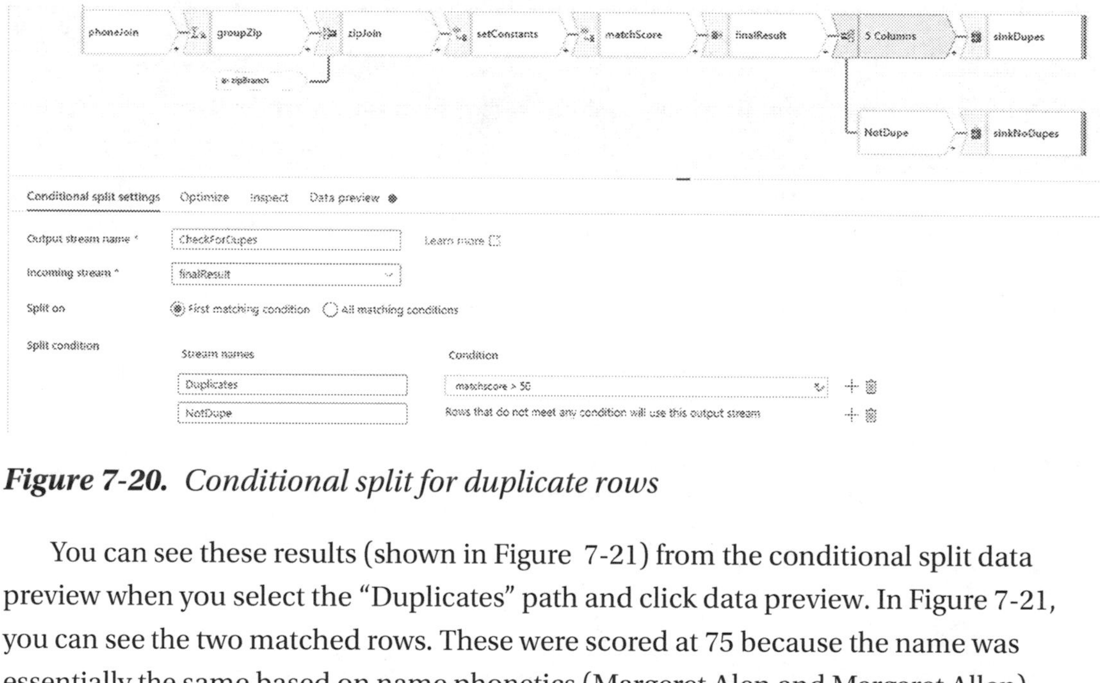

Figure 7-20. *Conditional split for duplicate rows*

You can see these results (shown in Figure 7-21) from the conditional split data preview when you select the "Duplicates" path and click data preview. In Figure 7-21, you can see the two matched rows. These were scored at 75 because the name was essentially the same based on name phonetics (Margeret Alen and Margaret Allen). Since the zip code was identical, our calculation of those two property matches scored high enough to send these rows down the duplicates path.

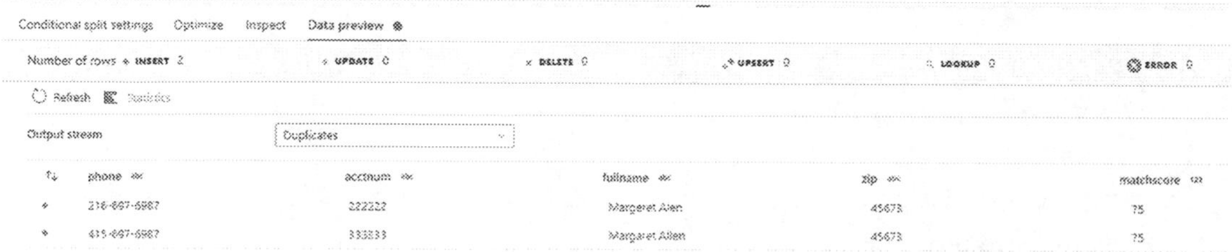

Figure 7-21. *Data preview of the duplicates path from the conditional split*

From the conditional split data preview, when you switch to "NotDupe", you will see all of the other rows from the employee data source including the remaining Margaret Allen from the three duplicate rows. Figure 7-22 is essentially a look at the cleaned data from the conditional split data preview.

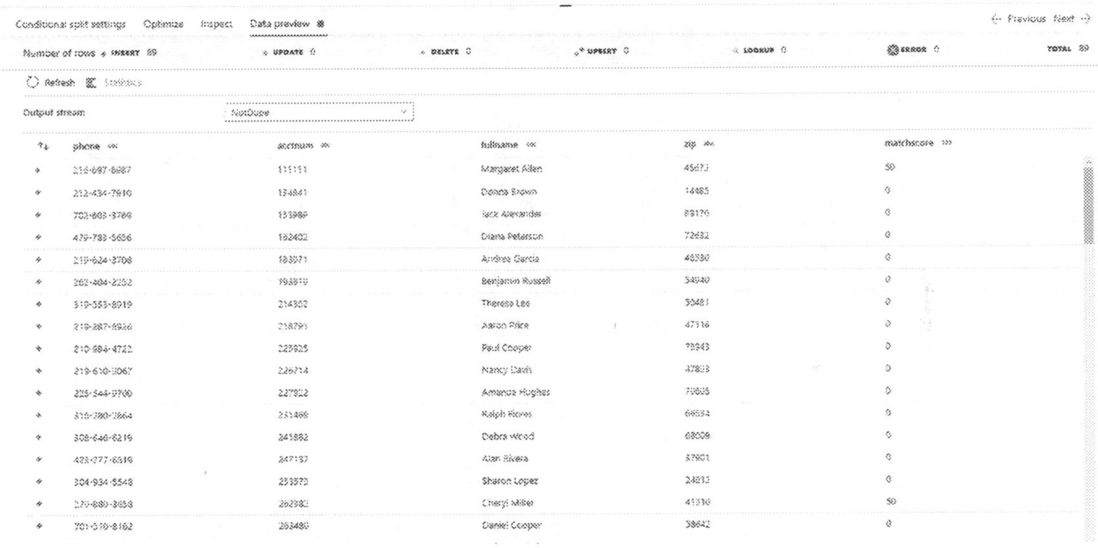

Figure 7-22. *Data preview of conditional split showing no duplicates*

Turn the Data Flow into a Reusable Flowlet

Now that we have a working deduplication data flow that has complex logic to it, we can turn it into a reusable transformation called a Flowlet. Think of a Flowlet as a data flow template with an input and output contract that you use to apply to different datasets. This way, we can use this same deduplication logic to other data flows without recreating the logic, and any changes that we make to the Flowlet will be applied everywhere that this transformation is being used.

The first thing to do is turn on the multiselect button on the Mapping Data Flow designer. Now you can draw a bounding box around all of the highlighted transformation nodes in the figure. Essentially, we want to turn everything, except for the original data flow's source and sink, into the templated Flowlet. Right-click and select "Create a new Flowlet" (Figure 7-23).

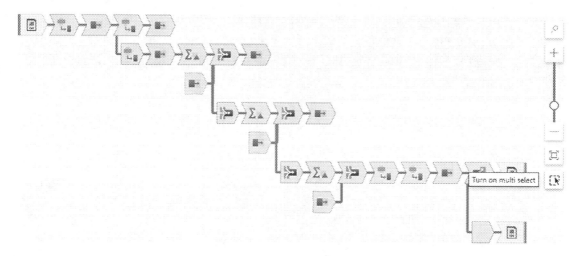

Figure 7-23. *Highlighted transformations to turn into a Flowlet using multiselect in the ADF UI*

ADF will automatically navigate to a new design tab that represents your new Flowlet. I changed the name to "DedupeFuzzyFlowlet1". You'll notice a few new transformation types appear as the source and sink. The original sources are replaced with Input transformations, and sinks are replaced with Output transformations. Inputs and Outputs are only valid inside flowlets. All they do is establish the column name and data type contracts that will be used by the consuming data flow where you will apply this new transformation Flowlet.

In the sample data flow shown earlier, we used a select transformation to create a semantic model with five properties that are used to first create a full name and then match on ID, phone number, and zip. Those properties are represented here in the Input transformation (Figure 7-24). The Output transformation uses auto-mapping like you've already seen in earlier chapters so that all columns are sent as output to the next transformation. You can also optionally map columns individually in the Output transformation.

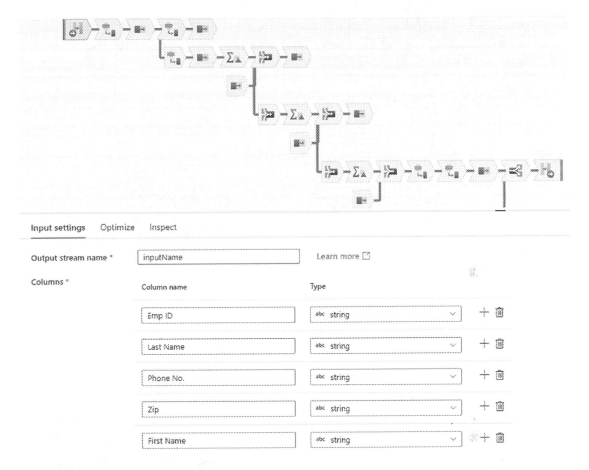

Figure 7-24. *Input mapping sets the incoming data contract for your Flowlet*

Debugging a Flowlet

Before we use this Flowlet inside of another data flow, we should test it inside the Flowlet designer. Debugging a Flowlet is a bit different than debugging a data flow. While you can use datasets for source data inside your Flowlet, the more common case is what we are doing here in this example, where we use Input transformations. The Input is akin to a function signature. Essentially, it is defining the contract for the incoming columns that will feed data into your Flowlet. Since there is not an actual dataset connected, you need to manually enter sample values and debug using those values. Also, data preview will only appear on the Output transformation. Click on data preview on the Output transformation, and then click Debug Settings. This is where you can enter values for your testing (Figure 7-25). Note that this Flowlet is taken from the deduplication data flow shown earlier, which had two separate sinks, one from each of the conditional split streams. When we turned it into a Flowlet, each sink became an output transformation.

Debug Settings

General   Parameters

Data flow debug IR: AutoResolveIntegrationRuntime

∨ inputName

inputName

＋ New   🗑 Delete

	Emp ID	First Name	Last Name	Phone No.	Zip
	abc	abc	abc	abc	abc

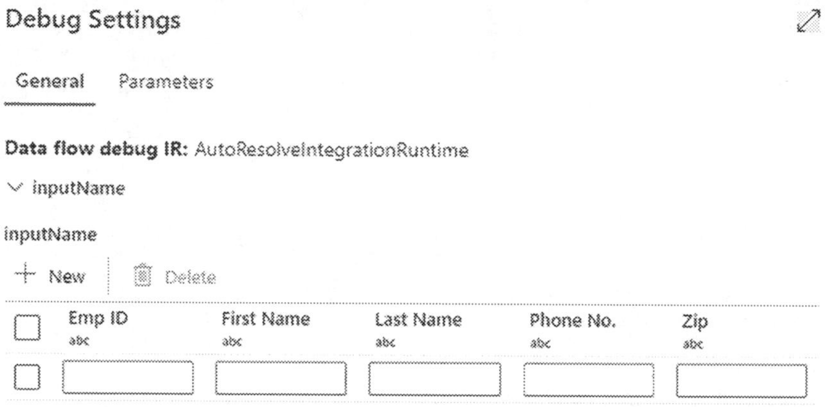

Figure 7-25. *Manually enter values to debug the Flowlet from the output transformation*

Once our testing has passed in debug mode and we're satisfied with the results, we can use this Flowlet as a custom transformation template in another data flow. To add a Flowlet, select "Flowlet" from the transformations toolbox (Figure 7-26) inside of another data flow. Select "DedupeFuzzyFlowlet1" from the available Flowlets selector, and now you've added your own custom transformation template to your data flow (Figure 7-27). It's that easy to add the same logic into any of your data flows which will make for a much more self-documented and easy-to-follow logical data flow.

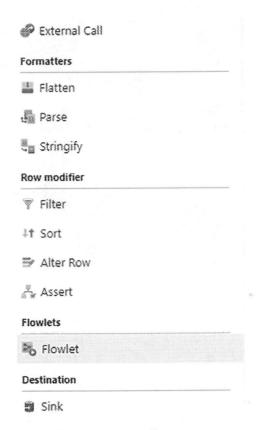

Figure 7-26. *Flowlet on transformation toolbox*

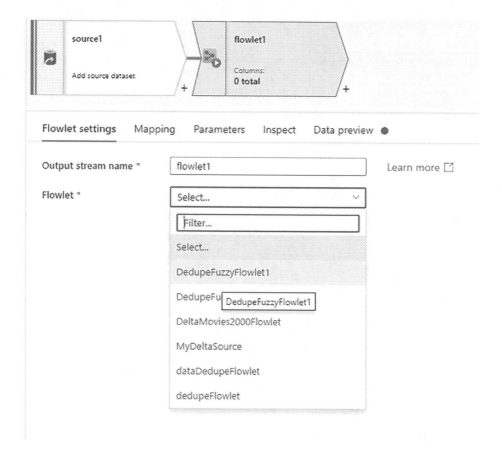

Figure 7-27. *Select the DeddupeFuzzyFlowlet1 from the Flowlet drop-down*

The final step to make your Flowlet work inside another data flow is to map the incoming column names in your data flow metadata to the input and output contracts from your Flowlet (Figure 7-28). Now each of those columns from your parent data flow will map to the associated input columns in your Flowlet.

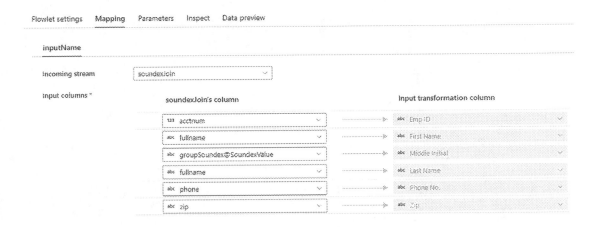

Figure 7-28. Mapping incoming data flow columns to the inputs on your Flowlet

Summary

In this chapter, we continued our exploration of ETL patterns in ADF using Mapping Data Flows. We used data transformation types like conditional split, aggregate, join, select, and flowlets. We also used expression functions including md5(), sha2(), and columnNames() to define distinct row and data deduplication data flows. We then turned a data flow into a Flowlet so that it can be reused in other data flows as a transformation template. In the next chapter, we're going to shift gears a bit into operationalizing our ETL pipelines using ADF's CI/CD capabilities and scheduling the pipelines for unattended execution.

CHAPTER 8

Mapping Data Flow Advanced Topics

This is the final chapter in Part II of this book where we are focusing on scalable ETL jobs with Mapping Data Flows. As opposed to the previous chapters in this section, where we used sample scenarios to describe data flow functionality, in this chapter, we're going to dive deep into three advanced topics on their own with new examples. These are all important topics that you will likely come across when processing massive amounts of data contained in data lakes in the cloud.

Working with Complex Data Types

For the most part, the samples that we've worked through so far have been performed using standard delimited text file formats and standard tabular data. However, you will also commonly come across data with complex data types: hierarchical structures, arrays, maps, etc. In this topic, I'm going to focus on how to transform and shape data of complex data types. In terms of which data lake file formats and data stores to watch out for that will contain these data structures, we'll talk more about it in the next topic. But for this topic of complex data types, you are likely to encounter these types in files of type JSON, Avro, Parquet, and Cosmos DB.

One important note on arrays and map data types in ADF: Datasets cannot read or write complex data types, meaning that you cannot use ADF pipeline activities like Copy with these structures. Instead, use Mapping Data Flows without a schema in your dataset. Leave the schema blank in your dataset and instead use "import projection" in the source Projection tab, or use the inline dataset option in the data flow source.

© Mark Kromer 2022
M. Kromer, *Mapping Data Flows in Azure Data Factory*, https://doi.org/10.1007/978-1-4842-8612-8_8

Hierarchical Structures

Let's first look at how to consume hierarchical data, and then we'll talk about how to generate hierarchies in ADF Mapping Data Flows.

Working with an Existing Hierarchical Structure

For the first example, I'm going to pull weather data for my region using the US National Weather Service REST API: `https://api.weather.gov/gridpoints/SEW/124,67/forecast`. Since this book focuses on ETL and data transformation, let's transform this hierarchical JSON data into a tabular form that can be stored as a CSV text file in the data lake to be consumed downstream, ostensibly by tools that cannot work with hierarchical data.

I created a REST source in my mapping data flow and pointed the Linked Service to that API (Figure 8-1).

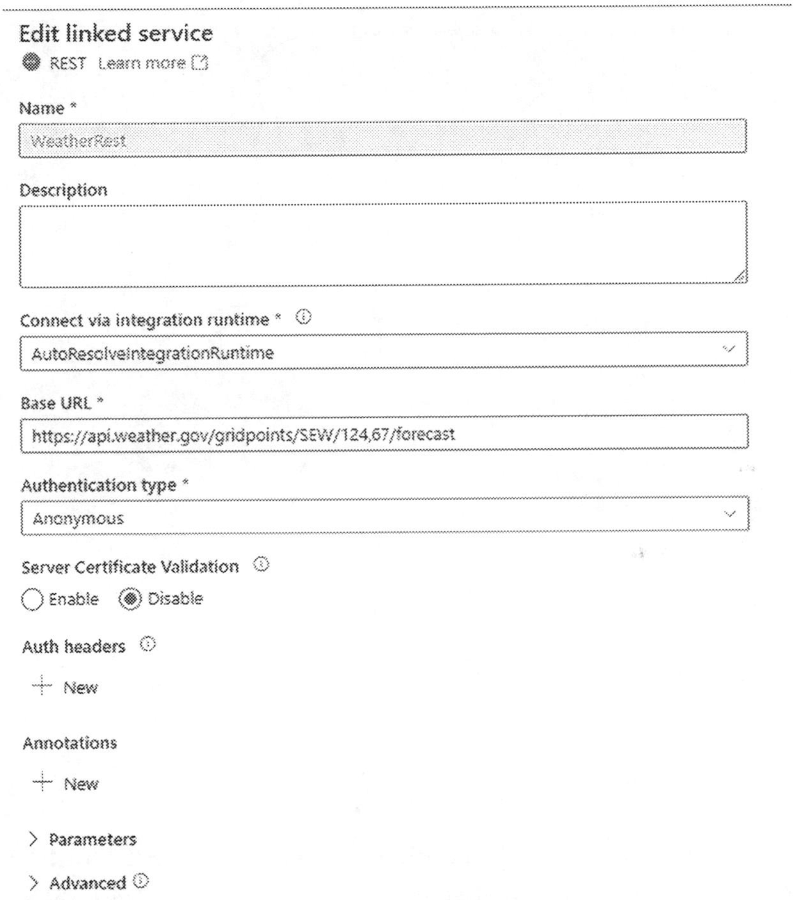

Edit linked service

REST Learn more

Name *

WeatherRest

Description

Connect via integration runtime * ⓘ

AutoResolveIntegrationRuntime

Base URL *

https://api.weather.gov/gridpoints/SEW/124,67/forecast

Authentication type *

Anonymous

Server Certificate Validation ⓘ

○ Enable   ◉ Disable

Auth headers ⓘ

+ New

Annotations

+ New

> Parameters

> Advanced ⓘ

Figure 8-1. *REST Linked Service for US National Weather Service*

To view the schema returned by the web service, click on "Import Schema" on the source transformation. A sample of the schema is shown in Figure 8-2. The output will be a JSON document with structures and arrays included in the schema.

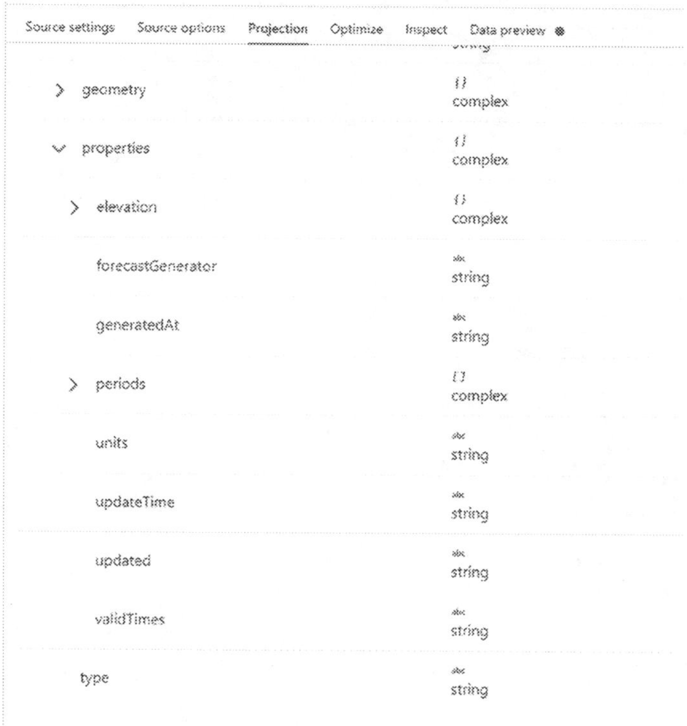

Figure 8-2. *Sample of REST Web API response schema*

What I'm looking to get out of this request is the weather forecast for time periods that is stored in the periods array. You can view the data returned from the web call in the source transformation when you click on data preview (see Figure 8-3). There is an array in this data called "periods" that contains the forecasts I want to send to my destination folder. To find the periods array in the data preview, you have to first click on the ADF visual indicator of hierarchical structure "{ ... }". From there, you'll be able to expand the array "periods" and view each of the values inside of the array indexes (Figure 8-3). Click on the array indicator [...] in the data preview panel to expand the array values.

Figure 8-3. *The periods forecast array*

Now that we know what the data will look like, let's get to the individual weather forecasts by unrolling the periods array into a denormalized tabular data table that can be written and consumed inside of a CSV text file sink. To do this, add a Flatten transformation after the source transformation (Figure 8-4).

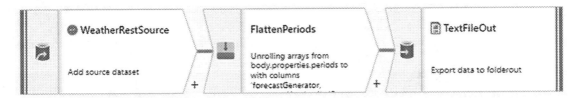

Figure 8-4. *Flatten transformation added after source*

In the Flatten settings, choose "body.properties.periods" for "Unroll by". Periods is the array to unroll, but it is inside of the properties structure under "body" (Figure 8-5).

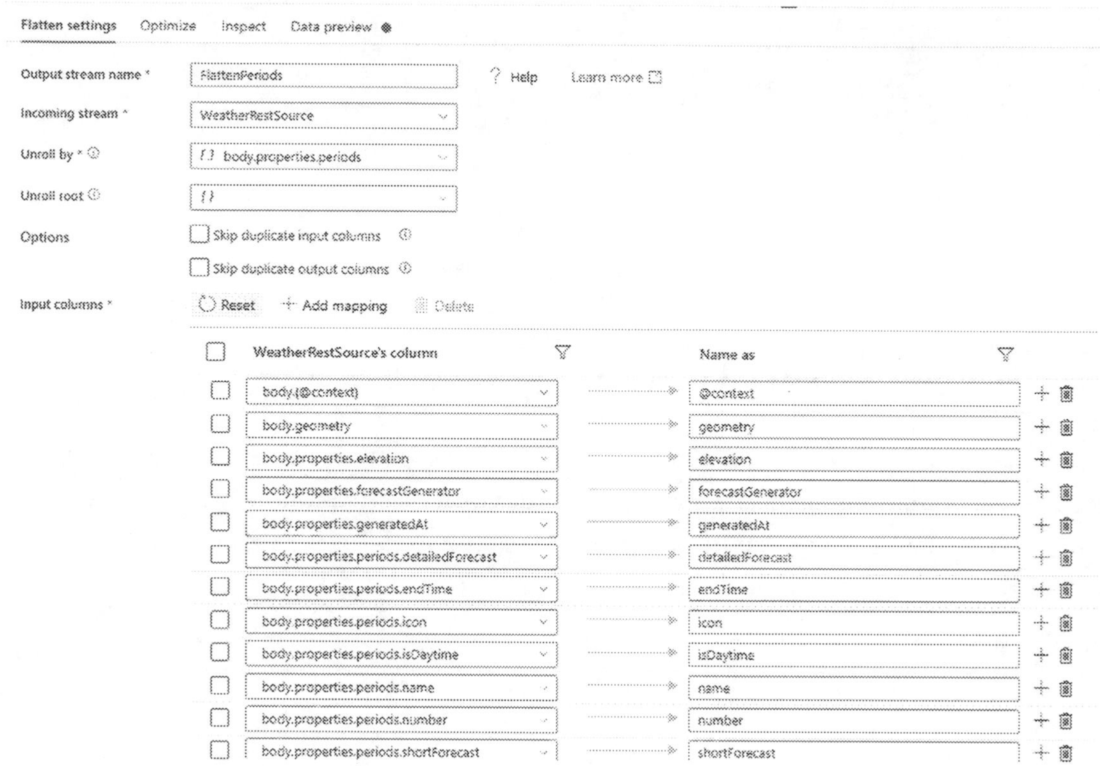

Figure 8-5. *Flatten transformation settings*

Click the "Reset" button on the Flatten transformation "Input columns" to reset the column projection whenever you change the unroll column. This will return a new row for every value found in the periods array, which will essentially denormalize the data. This is what we aim to do to make the data ready for a tabular output. However, clicking on the Inspect tab (output) in the Flatten transformation unveils three complex data types inside of the array still exist (Figure 8-6).

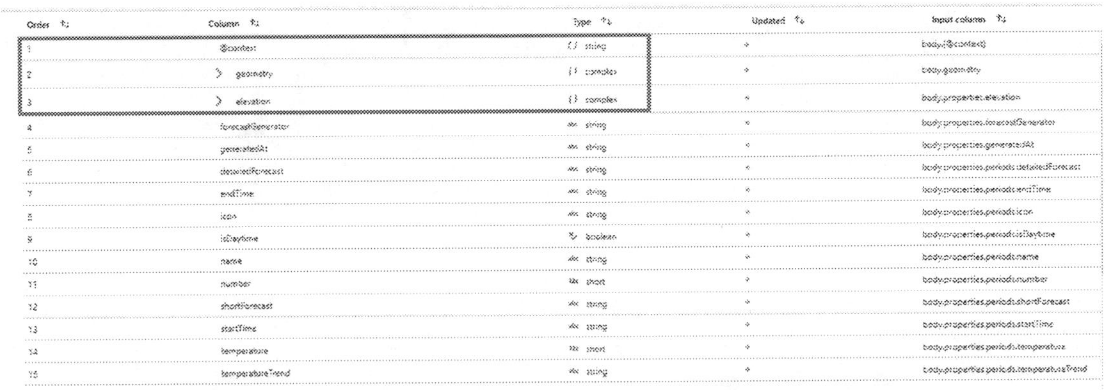

Figure 8-6. *Flatten Inspect shows three complex data types as output*

We can either further reduce those down to columns and rows or ignore them if we expect to consume those by a delimited text destination. For this example, we don't need them, so you can delete each of those three columns: context, which is a string array, and the structures geometry and the elevation columns from the input columns in the Flatten transformation settings. Once you do that, we should have an output that looks like the data preview from the Flatten transformation shown in Figure 8-7.

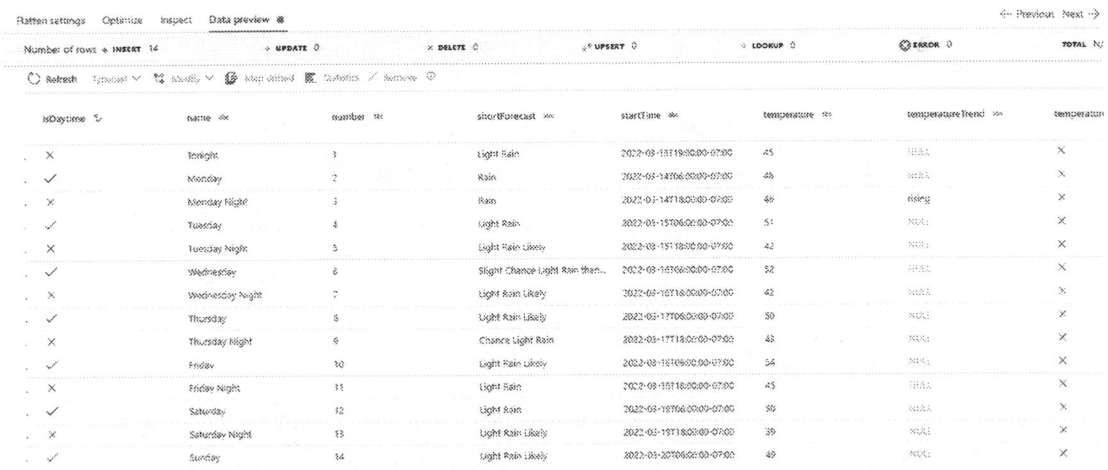

Figure 8-7. *Flattened array with no complex data types*

Removing the columns from the projection in the Flatten transformation is achieved by clicking on the Flatten settings tab and selecting the columns to delete under Input columns. You can then hit the Delete button from there as shown in Figure 8-8.

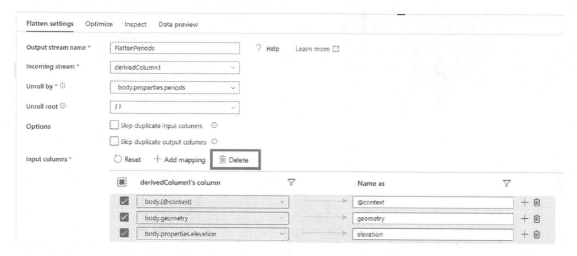

Figure 8-8. *Removing selected columns from the Flatten transformation to set a new projection*

Building a Structure

Let's shift gears and use ADF's Mapping Data Flow designer to build a structure and an array.

1. Add a Derived Column transformation. You will use the derived column to design hierarchies.

2. Take the flattened properties from the array unroll and create your own structure. Start by calling the new structure as "forecast".

3. There will be one level inside the hierarchy where we will store the name, shortForecast, and temperature from the incoming data. To create this structure, click the "Add subcolumn" button from the top-level hierarchy name (see Figure 8-9).

4. Inside of each property, click in the Expression panel and select the corresponding column name from the Expression values Input schema list.

Your finalized hierarchical structure would look like Figure 8-9. The results in data preview are shown in Figure 8-10.

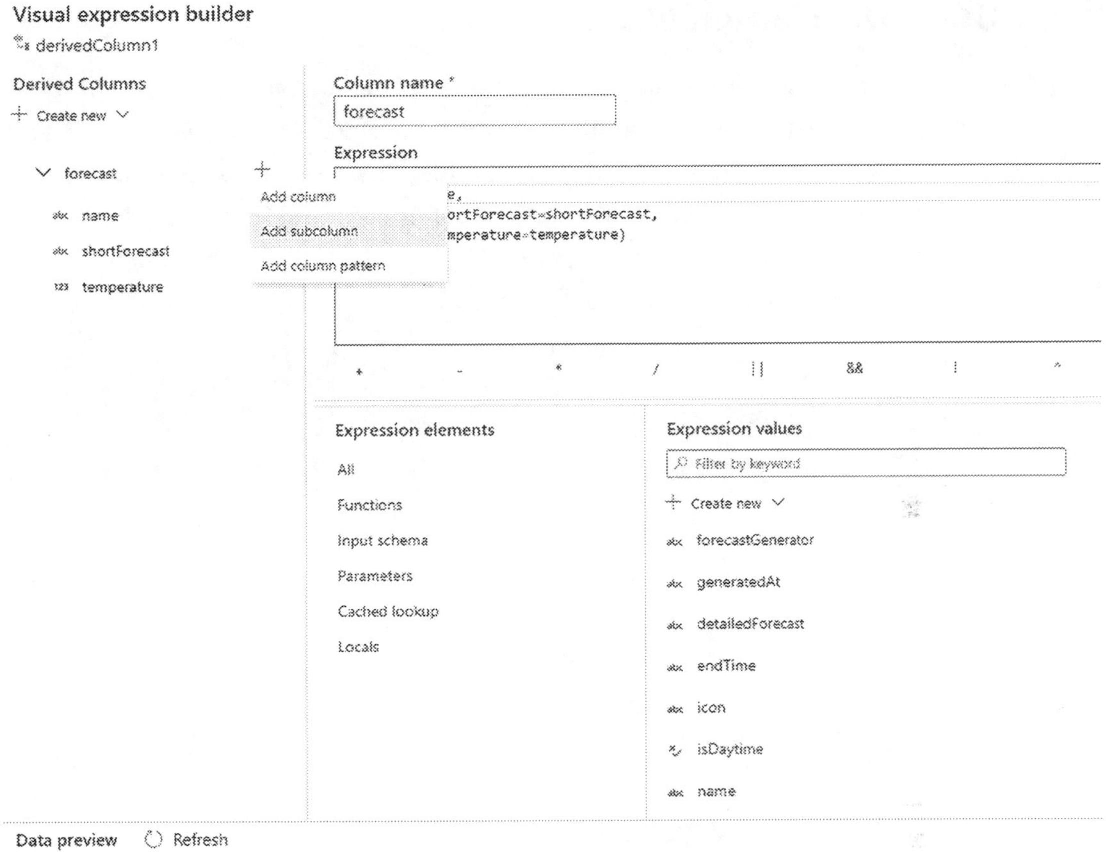

Visual expression builder

⁎⌐ derivedColumn1

Derived Columns		Column name *

+ Create new ⌄

forecast

⌄ forecast

	Expression

  + Add column

  abc name   Add subcolumn

  abc shortForecast Add column pattern

  123 temperature

e,
ortForecast=shortForecast,
mperature=temperature)

+   -   *   / || &&   :   ^

Expression elements	Expression values
All	🔍 Filter by keyword
Functions	+ Create new ⌄
Input schema	abc forecastGenerator
Parameters	abc generatedAt
Cached lookup	abc detailedForecast
Locals	abc endTime
	abc icon
	⤴ isDaytime
	abc name

Data preview   ↻ Refresh

Figure 8-9. *Creating forecast structure in derived column*

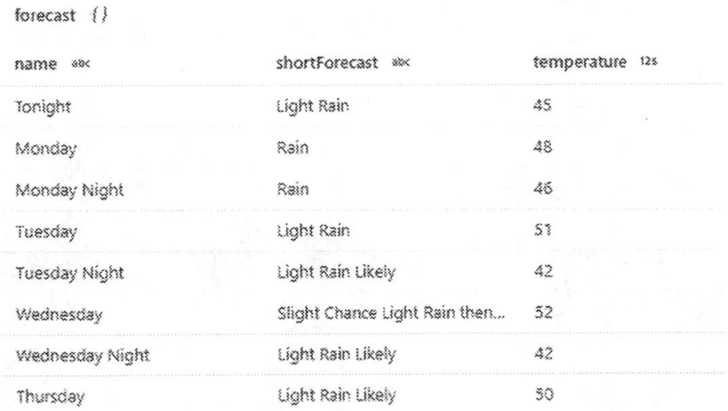

forecast { }

name abc	shortForecast abc	temperature 12s
Tonight	Light Rain	45
Monday	Rain	48
Monday Night	Rain	46
Tuesday	Light Rain	51
Tuesday Night	Light Rain Likely	42
Wednesday	Slight Chance Light Rain then…	52
Wednesday Night	Light Rain Likely	42
Thursday	Light Rain Likely	50

Figure 8-10. *The data preview results of our new hierarchical structure*

Using Other Transformations

There are two other important transformations for complex data types that you'll find under "Formatters" (see Figure 8-11) in the ADF Mapping Data Flows toolbox: Parse and Stringify. Use Parse when you have structures embedded inside of text strings in your source data. You can apply the desired hierarchical schema output in Parse. Stringify will allow you to take a structure and turn it into a single string that can be consumed downstream by a web service or tabular destination.

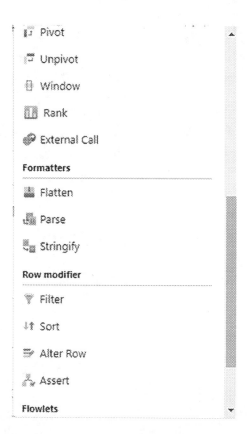

Figure 8-11. *The Mapping Data Flows toolbox showing Formatters category used for working with complex data structures*

Arrays

Arrays are common complex data structures that you'll work with in Mapping Data Flows. In this section, I'll show you how you can build your own arrays and how to decompose arrays from your source data.

Build an Array

To build an array in Mapping Data Flows, you'll use an Aggregate transformation with the collect() expression function. Let's walk through the process of building an array.

Let's say we want to take each of the weather forecasts and aggregate them into a single array so that we can send a single payload to REST endpoint as the sink.

1. Add an Aggregate transformation called "CollectForecasts" (see Figure 8-12).

2. Call the new columns as "forecasts". This will add a new top-level array to your metadata called "forecasts[]" that is an array of forecasts.

3. In the aggregate expression, collect the forecasts into an array by setting the expression to this value: `collect(forecast)`.

The new results are shown in Figure 8-13 by clicking on the Data Preview tab in the Aggregate transformation and then hovering over the new array we created called "forecasts".

Figure 8-12. *The chapter's hierarchical data flow with aggregation added for creating a new array*

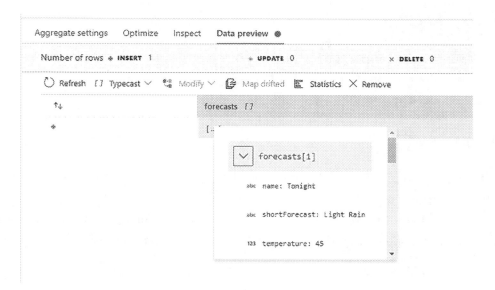

Figure 8-13. *Aggregate of forecasts as a new array*

Work with an Existing Array

We saw how to unroll arrays to denormalize the data for tabular output earlier. Now let's take a closer look at working with arrays in data flow expressions. There are many functions available to you as an ADF developer to manipulate arrays. We've already walked through how to create and unroll arrays. So now let's focus on a few of the most common array operations.

For these examples, you will use a derived column and the new forecasts array we created earlier. Take notice of the "#item" syntax in the following text. Item is a special reserved word that can be used in array expressions to represent the current item in the array as ADF loops through the array elements. In this case, the #item iterator can be appended with the properties in the array structure in order to match on the "name" property. Additionally, you can use #item1 and #item2 to compare the current item in the array iterator with the next item.

Here is a list of the most common operations you'll use inside ADF's data flow expression language when working with array data:

1. Sorting array elements

    Let's take the name property from the forecasts array and sort it alphabetically. To do so, use the #item syntax for current iterator and comparisons:

```
sort(map(forecasts, lower(#item.name)), compare(#item1,
#item2))
```

2. Modifying array elements

    Let's uppercase all of the name string elements in one shot inside the forecasts array:

    ```
    map(forecasts ,upper(#item.name))
    ```

3. Get array indexes

    You can retrieve and change the indexes used for array elements using "mapIndex". Notice the #index keyword that represents the array index:

    ```
    mapIndex(forecasts,#index)
    ```

4. Combine array values

    If you wanted to combine each of the forecasted temperatures into a single string value, use the reduce function and the #acc accumulator:

    ```
    reduce(array(toString(forecasts.temperature)), 'All
    Forecasts:', #acc + #item, #result)
    ```

    Result:
    All Forecasts:[48,46,51,42,52,42,50,44,53,44,51,39,49,40]

5. Filter and find values

    Let's say you are only interested in tonight's forecast. In the forecasts array, the name property contains the word "Tonight". You can find or filter for "Tonight" inside the array by using this syntax:

    ```
    find(forecasts,#item.name=='Tonight')
    filter(forecasts,#item.name=='Tonight')
    ```

6. Extract a subset of values

    This will extract just the first element in the forecasts array (starting with element 1 and ending with element 1):

    ```
    slice(forecasts,1,1)
    ```

Maps

Maps are a key/value (KV) representation of data where you can associate a value with a key for fast data lookup and organization. You will find map data types commonly in JSON and Parquet files.

Create a New Map

Let's start by creating a new KV map that will answer three primary common weather forecast questions: when, where, and what is the prediction as keys:

```
associate('When',name,'Where',generatedAt,'What',shortForecast)
```

Add that expression to a Derived Column and call the new column "forecastmap". Notice the map column data type indicator in the column header of data preview in Figure 8-14. When you hover over that column value, you'll be able to zoom into the contents of your map.

Figure 8-14. *Data preview of a map data type*

Now that we have a map (forecastmap), we can use the "reassociate" function to change any values inside of the map. Let's change the Where key to Pennsylvania for all map values: `reassociate(forecastmap, iif(#key=='Where','PA',#value))`. This example illustrates the use of the special keywords #key and #value to represent the current KV iterator for each element in the map.

Data Lake File Formats

As you learned earlier in this book, the ETL process takes raw data points and turns them into meaningful data in a data warehouse for business reporting. That refinement process in the cloud with data lakes is very similar to on-prem traditional ETL processes with a number of differences. In data lakes, data will vary greatly from day to day, there will be a general lack of upstream data quality, and the volume can grow enormously. That means that, as a data engineer focused on the ETL process, by the time you are designing your data flows in ADF, you cannot assume that the data will be of a specified format, shape, or size and you should not assume that the data is of a quality standard required for processing. For this first topic, let's focus on a few of the primary data formats that you will work with in the lake.

Parquet

This is very effective at storing massive amounts of data for analytics. Parquet is a columnar binary storage format that is also commonly compressed with gzip or snappy compression. For computing big data analytics in the lake using Spark, Parquet has become a de facto standard. ADF data flows, like most big data analytics platforms, utilize Spark as the compute engine, making Parquet a natural fit for processing data and partitioning with ETL processes. Writing Parquet to partitioned data lake folders is a very effective means for optimizing organization and reading data from the lake using Parquet. Partitioned writes are natively built into ADF on the Optimize tab in the Sink (Figure 8-15). As a binary format, Parquet contains metadata for each column but requires ADF, a reader client, or a compute environment in order to view the data.

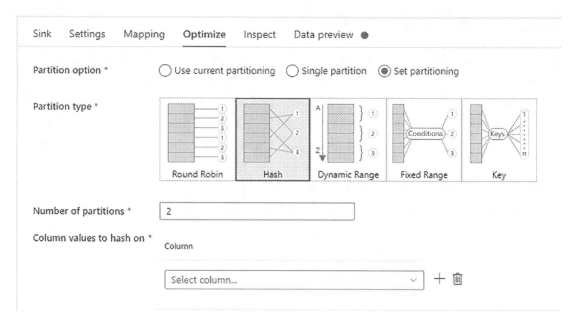

Figure 8-15. *Partitioned writes to the lake in the sink*

Delta Lake

Delta Lake was originally developed by Databricks and then eventually open sourced. It is a very common and emerging standard for providing an easy mechanism to provide CRUD operations and table partitioning using Parquet as the storage format. As a data engineer, working natively with Parquet, you are responsible for processing data updates, deletes, partitioning, etc. Delta provides a way to treat your data in Parquet folders and files essentially like tables. When you use Delta as a source or sink in ADF, your data will be stored as Parquet in partitioned folders in Azure Data Lake Store Gen2 (ADLS). Delta Lake manages data similar to a database using a transaction log.

Optimized Row Columnar

Like Parquet, **Optimized Row Columnar** (ORC) is a binary columnar format that was originally created for use by Hive and Hadoop and is found quite commonly in cloud data lake and big data analytics scenarios. In ADF, ORC can be used both as a source and a sink.

Avro

Avro format is a row-based storage format that you will see commonly emitted from serialization platforms like Azure Event Hubs and Apache Kafka. Avro stores data in JSON format, so you will use the hierarchical structure handling formats shown earlier in ADF.

JSON and Delimited Text

I'm going to group JSON and delimited text together because they are both very common file formats that exist outside of the data lake as well. With the exception of document data stores like Cosmos DB, incoming JSON data in ADF data flows will also be stored in readable text files similar to delimited text. Both delimited text and JSON files do not contain data types and metadata like Parquet and ORC. The primary difference between JSON and delimited text files is that JSON is formatted key value structures whereas delimited text files are stored as flat tabular data with column and row delimiters.

Data Flow Script

When you are designing a mapping data flow, ADF is generating a data flow script behind the scenes. When you execute your data flow from a pipeline activity, ADF uses that data flow script to define the logical intent of your transformation graph. You can manually edit the code behind your graph from the ADF UI, and you can also generate scripts that you can submit as data flow jobs using the ADF SDK. ADF takes the data flow script defined by your graph and bundles that as a payload to the Spark cluster execution service. You can always see the script behind your graph by clicking on the "Script" button from the designer UI (Figure 8-16). The following is a brief introduction to data flow script.

Figure 8-16. *Click on the script button on the top right of the Mapping Data Flow designer to work directly with the script behind the graph*

The script is composed of your named transformation streams with the name listed after "~>" at the end of the node definition. The edges are defined by putting the name of the transformation stream at the left-hand start of each new transformation definition. Directly after the name of the incoming stream is the type of transformation. For example:

```
Flatten1 window(newcol = last(1)) ~> window1
```

That script line defines a new node of type window called window1 with the Flatten1 transformation as in the input stream.

Let's take a look at two examples of data flow script starting with Figure 8-17. This example has five transformation nodes: source, aggregate, unpivot, sort, and sink. The source "source1" has a projection defined in the output clause of the source definition. The sink has schema drift enabled and schema validation turned off. Additional mappings and optimization settings would appear inside each of the script segments if there were set in the UI. The top-to-bottom ordering of the script does not necessarily equate to the linear left-to-right graph orientation in the UI. ADF will pass through the entire script and find each relationship throughout the script file before rendering the connected graph based on the configurations contained inside.

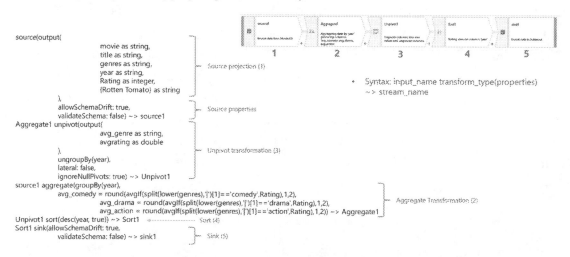

Figure 8-17. *Sample data flow script with source, aggregate, unpivot, sort, and sink*

Figure 8-18 represents a distinct values data flow with the optimize setting in the sink set to single has partitioning. The aggregate transformation ("DistinctRows") is using a column pattern that matches on the internal ADF metafunction "name".

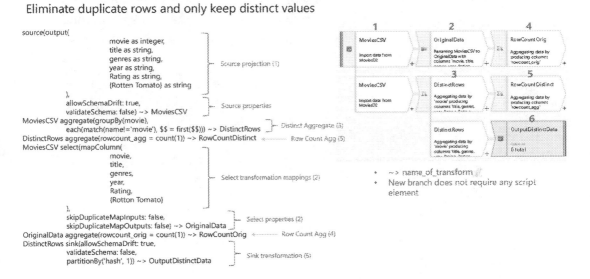

Eliminate duplicate rows and only keep distinct values

Figure 8-18. *Sample data flow script with source, select, aggregate, new branch, and sink*

You can use ADF APIs to define and execute data flows outside of the UI. To create a new data flow object, you must provide a complete, validated data flow script to the create API call. But you can still use the UI to define the data flow script to ensure it is validated. After designing the data flow, click the script button to view and edit the script. From that dialog box, click "Copy as single line" to save a version of script that is ready for JSON. ADF will reduce the script to a single line so that you can pass it to the API (Figure 8-19).

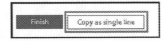

Figure 8-19. *Use the Copy as single line button on the bottom of the data flow script editor to use it inside of an API call*

Summary

In this chapter, you learned a few advanced topics for ADF Mapping Data Flows. We discussed how to handle complex data types like hierarchies, arrays, and maps. We discussed common data lake data formats and ADF's internal data flow script for defining your data transformations. This chapter was the final chapter in Part II, a deep dive into Mapping Data Flows. The final part of this book will focus on putting it all together into ADF pipelines and preparing your pipelines for operationalized production use.

PART III

Operationalize Your ETL Data Pipelines

CHAPTER 9

Basics of CI/CD and Pipeline Scheduling

Throughout the previous parts of this book, I sort of skipped over setting up a Git environment, implementing CI/CD processes, and scheduling of your pipelines in order to focus on the data flow logic. So let's now spend a chapter here to dive into setting up Git and scheduling your ETL jobs. These are both topics that are critically important to establishing your ADF ecosystem and to operationalize your data flows. Source code control, CI/CD, scheduling, and managing your factory pipelines are crucial for developing quality ETL processes, especially as your data environment grows over time. As we are focusing on low-code visual data transformations in this book, I'm only going to touch here on the basics of setting up Git for CI/CD processes in your factory and pipeline scheduling.

Configure Git

In each of the samples that I walked through earlier, I made sure to save my progress as I was going through the design and testing process inside the browser UI. In order to enable saving in your factory, you must configure a Git repo for your factory. Git is a very popular generalized process for managing source code. This process is built into ADF as Git integration. All you have to do is connect your factory to your organization's Git repos in GitHub or Azure DevOps.

There are two very important steps to put yourself into the best environment to develop ETL pipelines. The first is creating a new factory and then connecting to Git from the Azure portal. The second step is connecting an existing factory to Git. It is very important to connect your factory to Git so that you can save your work in a branch as your "scratch space." Without Git, ADF is forced to update the live service configurations of your pipelines and data flows, which will require a fully validated pipeline before you

139

© Mark Kromer 2022
M. Kromer, *Mapping Data Flows in Azure Data Factory*, https://doi.org/10.1007/978-1-4842-8612-8_9

can publish your work. In other words, there is no ability to save in place while designing in the UI without Git configured.

New Factory

Let's start at the very beginning of the process of creating a new data factory from the Azure portal (`https://portal.azure.com`) and connecting to an existing GitHub repo. Here are the steps to follow:

1. Log in to the Azure portal.

2. Click new resource ➤ Integration ➤ Data Factory (see Figure 9-1).

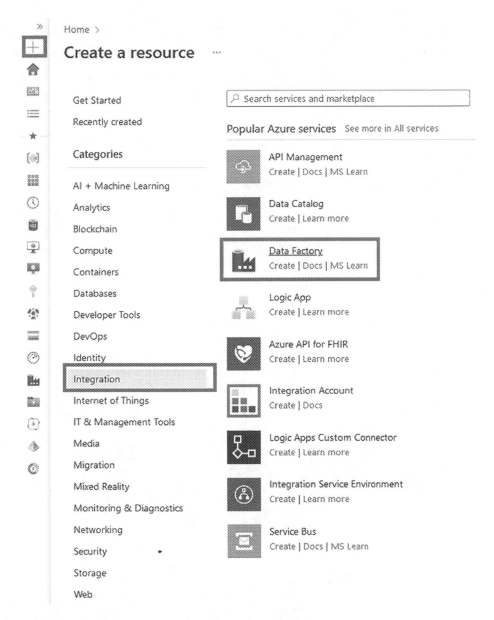

Figure 9-1. *Azure portal create new Data Factory*

3. Provide a name for your new factory while also picking the Azure
   region and resource group where your factory will be located (see
   Figure 9-2).

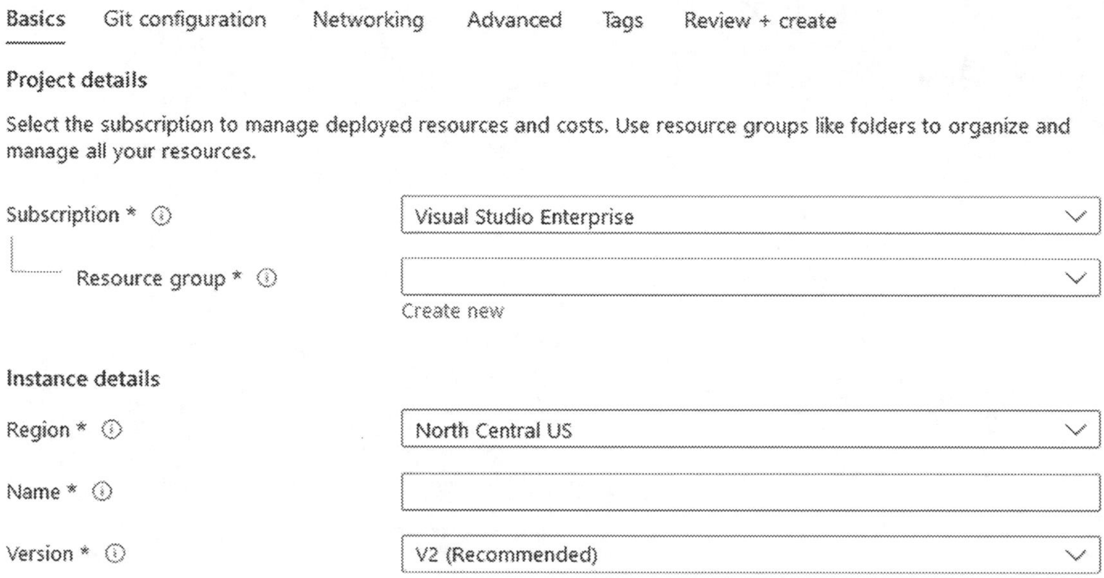

Basics   Git configuration   Networking   Advanced   Tags   Review + create

Project details

Select the subscription to manage deployed resources and costs. Use resource groups like folders to organize and manage all your resources.

Subscription * ⓘ | Visual Studio Enterprise   ∨ |

└──── Resource group * ⓘ | ∨ |
                                     Create new

Instance details

Region * ⓘ | North Central US   ∨ |

Name * ⓘ | |

Version * ⓘ | V2 (Recommended)   ∨ |

Figure 9-2. *Basic settings for a new data factory*

4. The next tab is "Git configuration". This is where I'll point to my Git repo in GitHub. The settings in Figure 9-3 are slightly different when you select Azure DevOps (ADO). We'll talk through setting up ADO for your ADF repo in the next section.

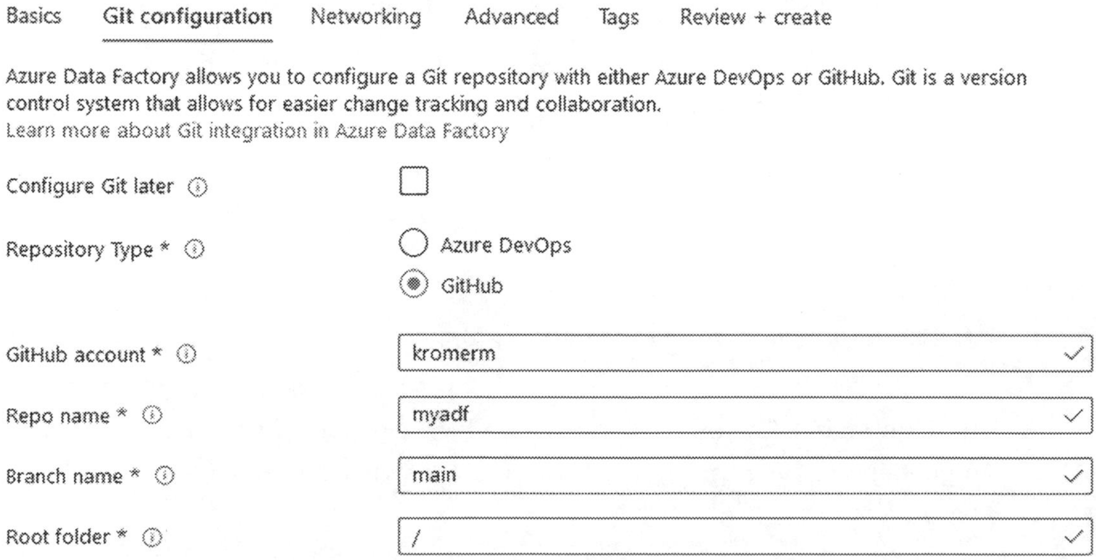

Basics   **Git configuration**   Networking   Advanced   Tags   Review + create

Azure Data Factory allows you to configure a Git repository with either Azure DevOps or GitHub. Git is a version control system that allows for easier change tracking and collaboration.
Learn more about Git integration in Azure Data Factory

Configure Git later ⓘ   ☐

Repository Type * ⓘ   ◯ Azure DevOps
                                    ◉ GitHub

GitHub account * ⓘ | kromerm   ✓ |

Repo name * ⓘ | myadf   ✓ |

Branch name * ⓘ | main   ✓ |

Root folder * ⓘ | /   ✓ |

Figure 9-3. *Git configuration for a new factory*

Existing Factory

If you already have a factory created, you can add or change the Git configuration for your factory. In this example, I'll walk through how to connect to Azure DevOps instead for the Git repo. Here's what to do:

1. Open your existing factory, and inside the ADF UI, click on the Manage ➤ Git configuration link.

2. Click configure and choose Azure DevOps Git for the type of code repository.

3. Select your DevOps organization, project, and repo name (see Figure 9-4).

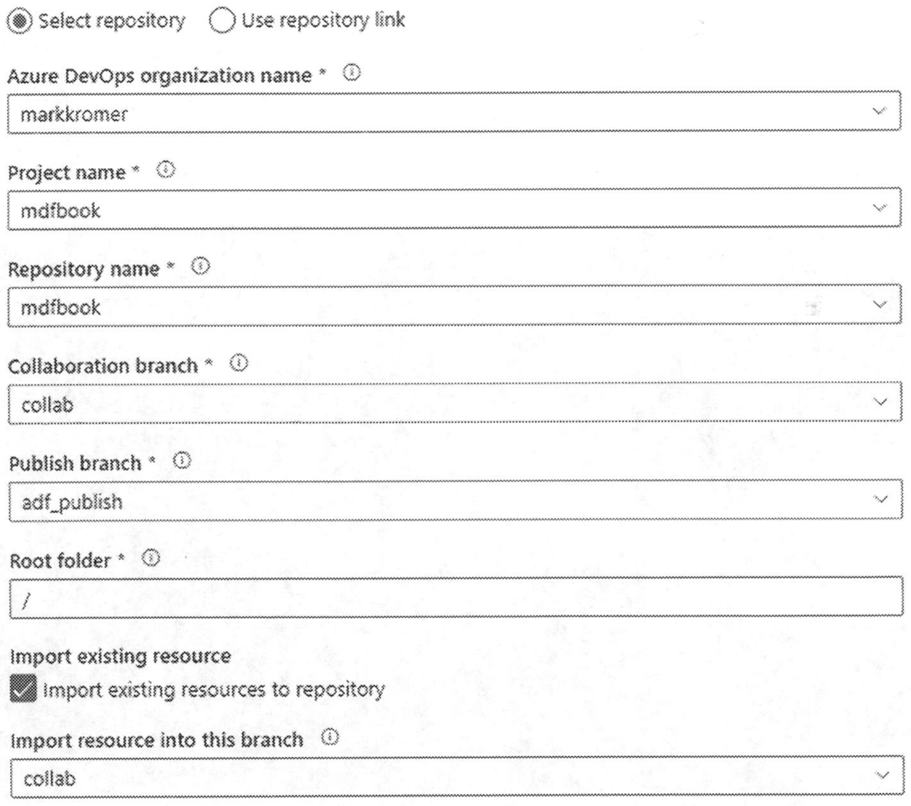

Figure 9-4. Configure Azure DevOps as the code repository service for an existing ADF factory

4. ADF will use the branch you select for "collaboration branch" as the branch that you will set in your ADF UI when you click "publish". Notice in my earlierexample, I used the name "collab" for my collaboration branch. This is intentionally different from the "main" branch, which is where I will publish from when collaborating on my factory with other developers.

5. The Publish branch is used as a special branch for ADF to store the ARM template that is generated in the background when publishing changes to the live service.

6. If you select "Yes" for "Import resource into this branch", ADF will import the existing ADF factory JSON definitions into the branch you've selected here.

ADF will store each of your ADF artifacts as a JSON file inside of your repo with folders representing each of the artifact types (see Figure 9-5). You can use your source control tool to look at diffs and manage branches. Inside of ADF, you can collaborate on a single factory with other users by using branching.

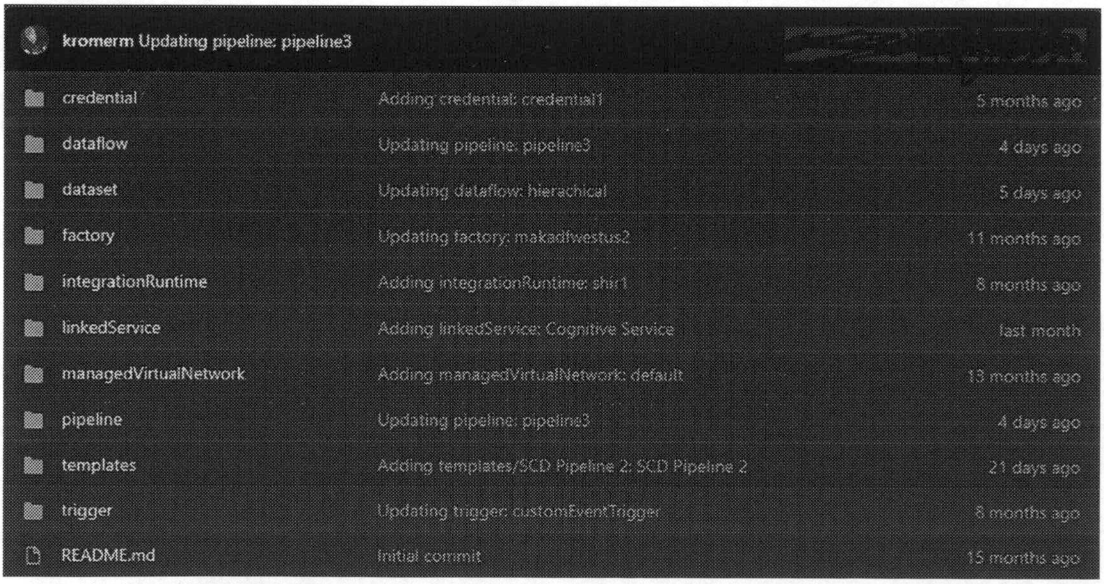

Figure 9-5. *Source folder for each of your factory resources, stored as JSON*

Branching

The Git process evolved as a software engineering code control tool. In ADF, we've brought Git to the DataOps world for data engineers. A key concept to learn is that when you begin work on a new set of changes to your factory, the best first step to take is to create a new branch. You can either create a new branch from your Git tool or you can click on New Branch from the ADF UI (Figure 9-6). The branch will act as each developer's "scratch space" to work on a factory and save the live changes without requiring deployment and publishing to the live service until all tests have passed.

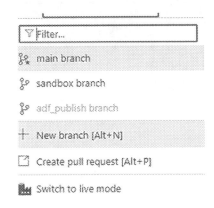

Figure 9-6. *Create new code branch in Git from ADF UI or select existing branch*

Note that the unit of work (or branch) in ADF is the entire factory. So when you create a new branch, all of the artifacts from your current factory are copied to the new branch. For example, if I create a new branch called "bookbranch", I can now create a new pipeline called "markpipe" and follow the rest of the CI/CD process manually. First, ensure that the new branch is the current active branch (see Figure 9-6 to view the current branch you are working on in your ADF UI). This is now a new sandbox area for your pipeline development and testing work. You can save your work and test it using the pipeline debug and data flow data preview.

Once your testing is complete, you can create a new pull request (shown in Figure 9-6). In Figure 9-7, you'll see an example where my changes in bookbranch will merge in the collab branch. You should have your pipeline collaborators review your changes before approving.

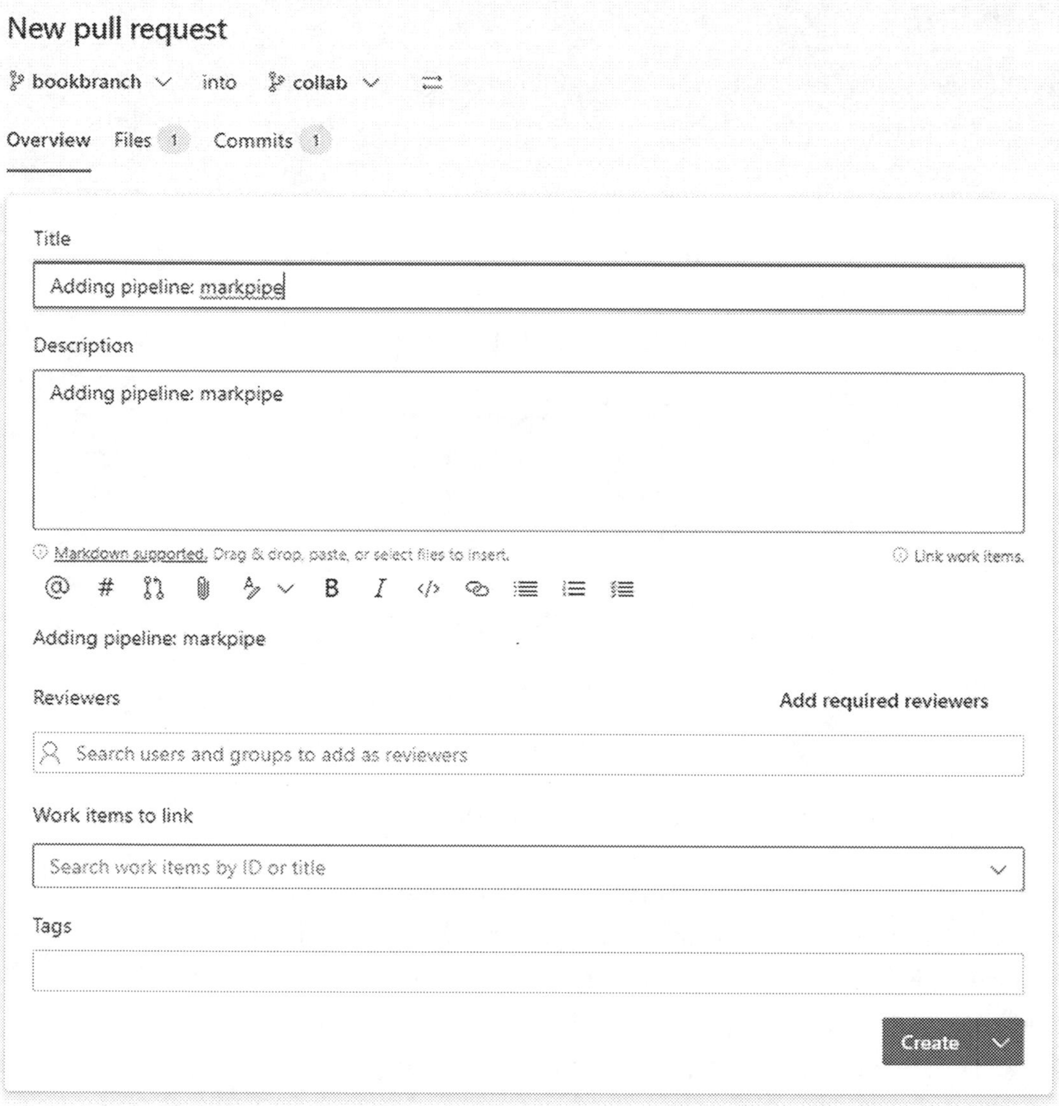

New pull request

⑂ bookbranch ∨   into   ⑂ collab ∨   ⇄

Overview   Files ①   Commits ①

Title

Adding pipeline: markpipe

Description

Adding pipeline: markpipe

ⓘ Markdown supported. Drag & drop, paste, or select files to insert.   ⓘ Link work items.

@   #   ⅋   📎   🖍 ∨   B   *I*   </>   🔗   ≣   ≔   ≣

Adding pipeline: markpipe

Reviewers   **Add required reviewers**

🔍 Search users and groups to add as reviewers

Work items to link

Search work items by ID or title   ∨

Tags

Create ∨

Figure 9-7. *Pull request form in Azure DevOps*

Once the PR has been approved, you can switch to the collab branch where you will
see your new pipeline, markpipe, in the ADF UI (Figure 9-8). All developers collaborating
on this factory will use this branch to push their changes into a common branch.
However, these changes are still only in staging ready for testing. After successful testing,
you have one more step to take to push this into the production live ADF service. You can
also now delete your working branch since the changes have been merged. The working

branch is a temporary scratch space that you'll delete when done and recreate whenever you begin working on new updates.

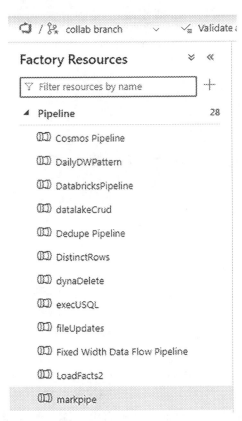

Figure 9-8. *Following the approval of your PR and the merge of your changes, you now see "markpipe" in the collab branch*

Publish Changes

The final step is to publish from the collab branch to the live service. I mentioned earlier that a branch contains the entire set of factory artifact JSON files. Factories can get quite complex and large, so it is a good idea to check that all objects are valid. When you are using Git with ADF, the repo is storing your work as files in folders, and they can include invalid configurations. Keep this in mind when determining when to segment your factory. If your factory size grows to hundreds of pipelines and other artifacts, it can be very cumbersome to manage the CI/CD process. It may be beneficial to split up your pipelines across multiple factories.

First, click Validate All to ensure that all artifacts are valid. If there are invalid objects, ADF will provide a list of the errors as shown in an example in Figure 9-9. You can click on the errors in the list and ADF will take you to the error in your factory.

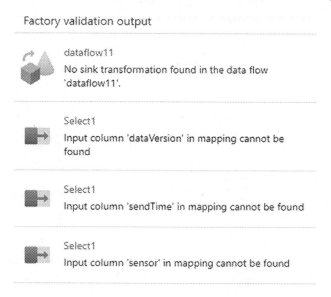

Figure 9-9. *Data factory validation errors when publishing*

Once all errors have been resolved, ADF will present you with a list of diffs between the current collab branch and the live service (Figure 9-10), which is represented by the special "publish branch" that is called adf_publish. ADF will automatically create the branch (adf_publish) and store the ARM templates used for exporting your data factory artifacts there.

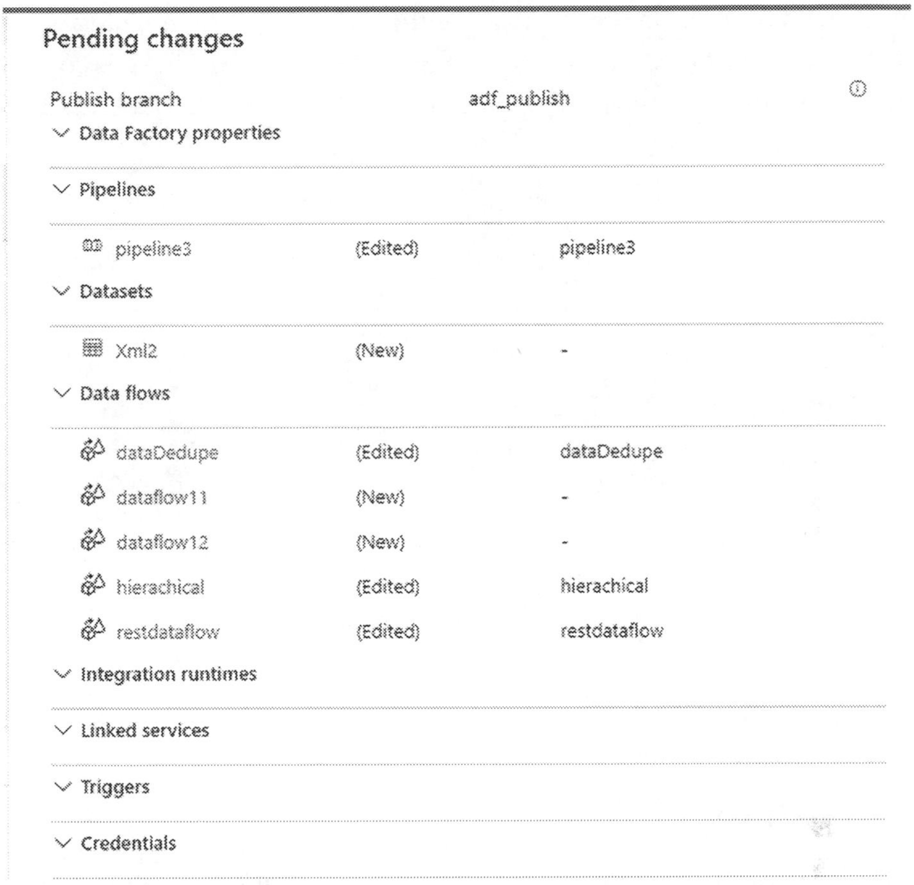

Figure 9-10. *Diffs from collab branch and live ADF factory*

It is worth noting that since your factory resources are stored as JSON files in the Git repo, you can also use your source control tool's diff mechanisms as shown in Figure 9-11.

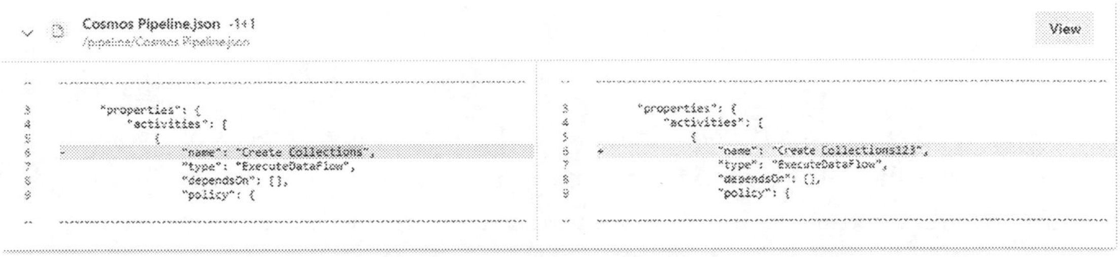

Figure 9-11. *Diffs of an ADF JSON pipeline artifact using Azure DevOps*

The final step is to click on the "Publish" button and publish your changes to the ADF service. Make sure that your current branch is "collab". Once the publish is complete, you will see the new factory version if you open a browser with the ADF UI pointed to "live mode" as shown in Figure 9-12.

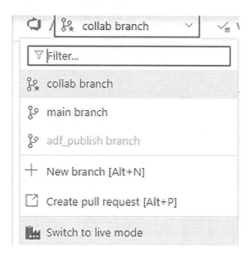

Figure 9-12. *ADF live mode*

Pipeline Scheduling

You can execute your ADF pipeline from the UI manually using the Debug button while unit testing your logic. You can also use the Trigger Now button to kick off a triggered execution of your pipeline. Both of these are immediate invocations of your pipeline as opposed to unattended trigger-initiated executions. Before we talk about the four trigger types in ADF for scheduling your ETL jobs, I want to touch on the differences between debug and trigger now runs and how they relate to ETL pipelines with data flows.

Debug Run

Before publishing your factory, it is recommended to run through a series of test cases first. You can use the debug button for that in the pipeline designer without publishing your factory. Although you cannot save your work when you are not connected to Git, you can still debug and then publish from the live service. However, it is recommended to always use the Git CI/CD process described in this chapter. When you are connected to Git, the debug button will allow you to interactively test pipelines from different branches.

Additionally, when you have a data flow activity in your pipeline, you will need to have an active debug session in order to have the Spark environment running on your Azure IR before your data flow can execute.

Trigger Now

The trigger now option in ADF allows you to execute your pipeline from the published live service version of your factory. ADF will immediately execute your pipeline. This option is handy when you wish to perform a sanity check on your factory after it has been published. Another good use of trigger now is when you test your data flows with sampled data using debug. A good final test would be to test the data flow in your pipeline harness after publishing. There is one other good use for this option, and that is when you create a single-use pipeline. If you do not need to set a regular cadence for your pipeline, then you can just trigger it manually from the UI.

One important point I want to point out with trigger now: Because it executes only published factory artifacts, the version of the factory being used is likely an older version from the version that you are editing in your branch.

Schedule Trigger

The schedule trigger is very popular in ADF and acts essentially like a wall-clock style trigger where you can set a start time, end time, and recurring cadence. Think of it as equivalent to an Outlook calendar schedule or a SQL Agent job. It is a very common trigger for most ETL jobs.

Tumbling Window Trigger

Tumbling window trigger generates buckets of time based on the recurrence that you set. You can also set a start time and an end time as well as dependencies on other tumbling window triggers. Tumbling window triggers are very powerful and have advanced features like delay start time and retry policies as well as facilities to handle overlapping window concurrency. A good use case for tumbling windows is when you have jobs that wait for data to arrive on an established cadence that will often require backfilling by using windows of time in the past and automatic retries.

Storage Events Trigger

Storage events triggers are very useful when your ETL job cannot rely on a time-based cadence or schedule. With this trigger type, you can execute your pipeline whenever a file arrives or is deleted in your storage account. Keep in mind that ADF is a batch-oriented data pipeline service. Event triggers in ADF do not make your pipeline a real-time live event consumer. If you receive thousands of files in an hour, you will reach your service limits and face pipeline failures and throttling. Instead, use this trigger type to kick off a pipeline based on files that will arrive a few times an hour. Another good practice is to use the concept of a trigger file. In this scenario, an external process will write a simple text file to the target folder location where you have set up the file event listener. The file does not contain data to be processed. Instead, think of a pattern where the storage trigger acts as a semaphore to kick off your pipeline.

Custom Events Trigger

The final type of trigger allows you to define custom events in Event Grid and connect to a topic as a listener. Whenever an event is received by Event Grid with a subject that you define in the trigger, your pipeline will be executed. Similar to the storage events trigger mentioned earlier, the custom events trigger instantiates a new pipeline execution upon every event received. So use the same good practices listed earlier in terms of event frequency when using this trigger.

You can create, edit, and manage your triggers in the ADF UI under Manage ➤ Triggers (Figure 9-13).

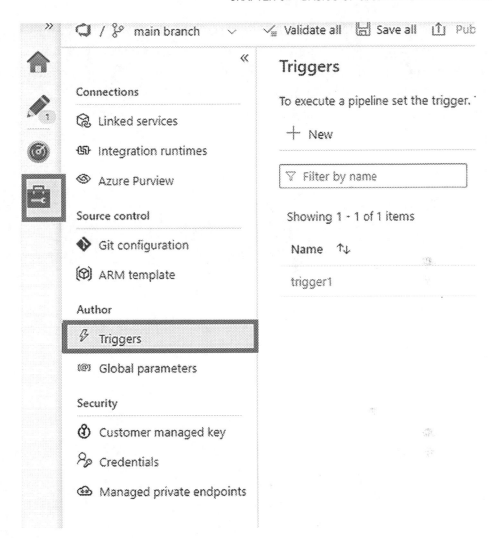

Figure 9-13. *Manage triggers from ADF UI*

Summary

In this chapter, we went back to the point of factory creation from the Azure portal to demonstrate how to configure Git and CI/CD for a new data factory. After configuring Git repos for collaboration and source control, we looked at operationalizing our pipelines with ADF triggers. When creating ETL data pipelines with data flows, it is very important to configure Git in your ADF to enable collaboration, CI/CD, and source control for you work. Even more fundamentally, integrating with Git in ADF enables the save operation in your branch, or scratch area, without the need to fully validate you data flow or other pipeline artifacts first. In the next chapter, we're going to take our completed ETL pipelines and monitor their execution life cycle and look at areas of optimization in terms of performance and reusability.

CHAPTER 10

Monitor, Manage, and Optimize

This chapter is going to cover a lot of ground. There is also an expectation that you've made your way through most of the earlier chapters and feel comfortable building ETL pipeline in ADF using Mapping Data Flows as by this part of the book, I'm going to make a number of assumptions in terms of your understanding of ADF and Mapping Data Flows.

After you've deployed and operationalized your factory, you'll want to monitor the health of your scheduled pipelines and data flows and look for ways to optimize your ETL jobs. In this chapter, I'm going to cover a range of topics that will help you to manage your factories from the ADF UI and understand how to tune performance based on the monitoring feedback. I would like you to think of two top-level categories when looking at performance optimizations in Mapping Data Flows:

1. Data flow activity (macro) performance: The effect that changing the size of your integration runtime will have on the compute that is utilized to execute your jobs

2. Data flow logical (micro) performance: Deep, detailed analysis of your data and the logic inside of your data flows as method to tackle bottlenecks that were uncovered through data profiling and analyzing your pipeline execution plans

Monitoring Your Jobs

Inside of your factory UI, you will see the monitoring icon in the left panel (see Figure 10-1). Clicking there will take you to the monitoring view (also Figure 10-1) where you will be able to view the status of your triggered pipelines as well as your debug runs and manual executions.

© Mark Kromer 2022
M. Kromer, *Mapping Data Flows in Azure Data Factory*, https://doi.org/10.1007/978-1-4842-8612-8_10

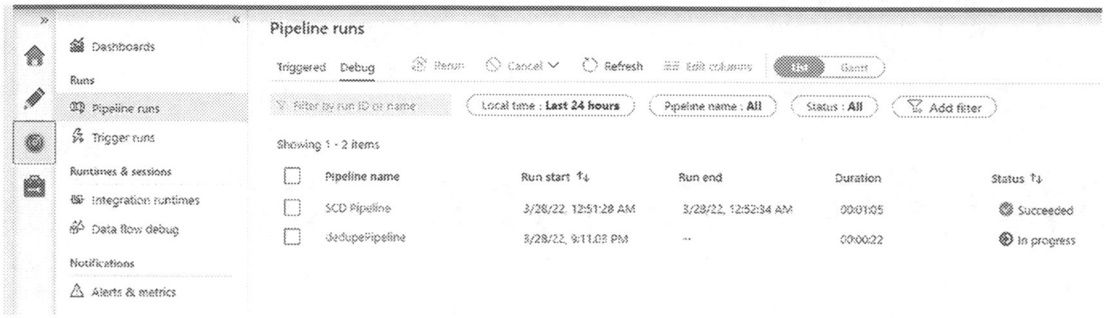

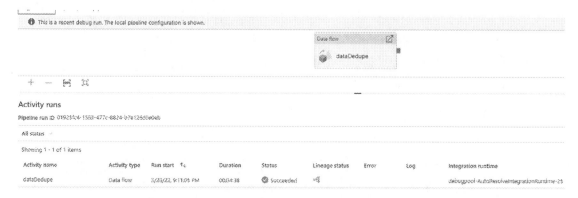

Figure 10-1. *ADF monitoring view*

You can view all your factory activity either by pipeline or by trigger. In this chapter, we're going to dive into how you can use the data flow execution plan as a way to evaluate and optimize your data flows. Earlier in the book, I showed how debug pipeline runs will display the pipeline execution results and deep data flow activity monitoring from the output tab on the pipeline designer. In the monitoring view, you can view the same information from both attended and unattended executions. Clicking into the pipeline "dedupePipeline" shown in the right pane of Figure 10-1, we navigate into the details of the pipeline execution (Figure 10-2).

Figure 10-2. *Activity details inside the pipeline monitoring view*

In this pipeline, I only have one activity. This is the dataDedupe data flow activity that we built earlier in the book. You can see the activity level details in the table in the bottom pane. We can see that it took 4 minutes and 38 seconds to execute my data flow activity and that it ran successfully, as well as which integration runtime was used for the activity execution. When you hover over the activity row in the bottom table, you will see an eyeglasses icon. Clicking that will give you details about the activity execution plan (Figure 10-3).

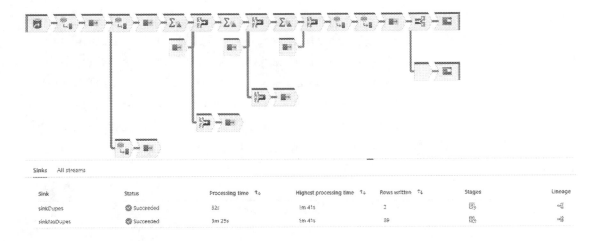

Figure 10-3. *Mapping Data Flow execution plan*

The display in Figure 10-3 is the ADF interpretation of the graph that was designed earlier for the data deduplication process. This view will tell you which nodes succeeded and which ones failed, as well as which nodes are currently processing based on the colored line on the top of each node. You can view the progress of your pipeline and data flows while they are in flight from this view. Clicking on each transformation will give you a view like you see in the sink detail view in Figure 10-4.

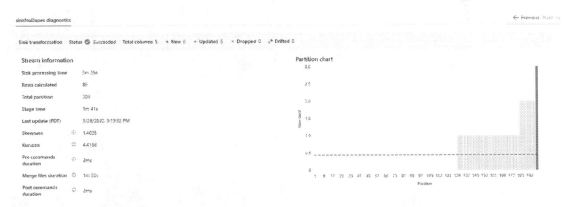

Figure 10-4. *Detailed view of the sink transformation*

The important detail in the sink in this example is that there were 200 partitions used in Spark when this data was processed. We did not explicitly set a partition value in the design, so this was used by default by Spark for this execution. If you add more cores to your integration runtime, ADF can further partition your data, unless you explicitly set the number of partitions in the Optimize tab available on each transformation. Take note of the total sink processing time of 3 minutes and 25 seconds in Figure 10-4. That is calculated by the "stage" of processing that is shown in Figure 10-5. When ADF receives your instructions for transformation, it is sent to the Spark executor. The Spark job interprets the data flow script payload and executes your transformation intent in an optimized way by creating stages of processes. When you look at the stages for your data flows, you'll see that the "TIME" column will represent that grouping of transformations that were performed together.

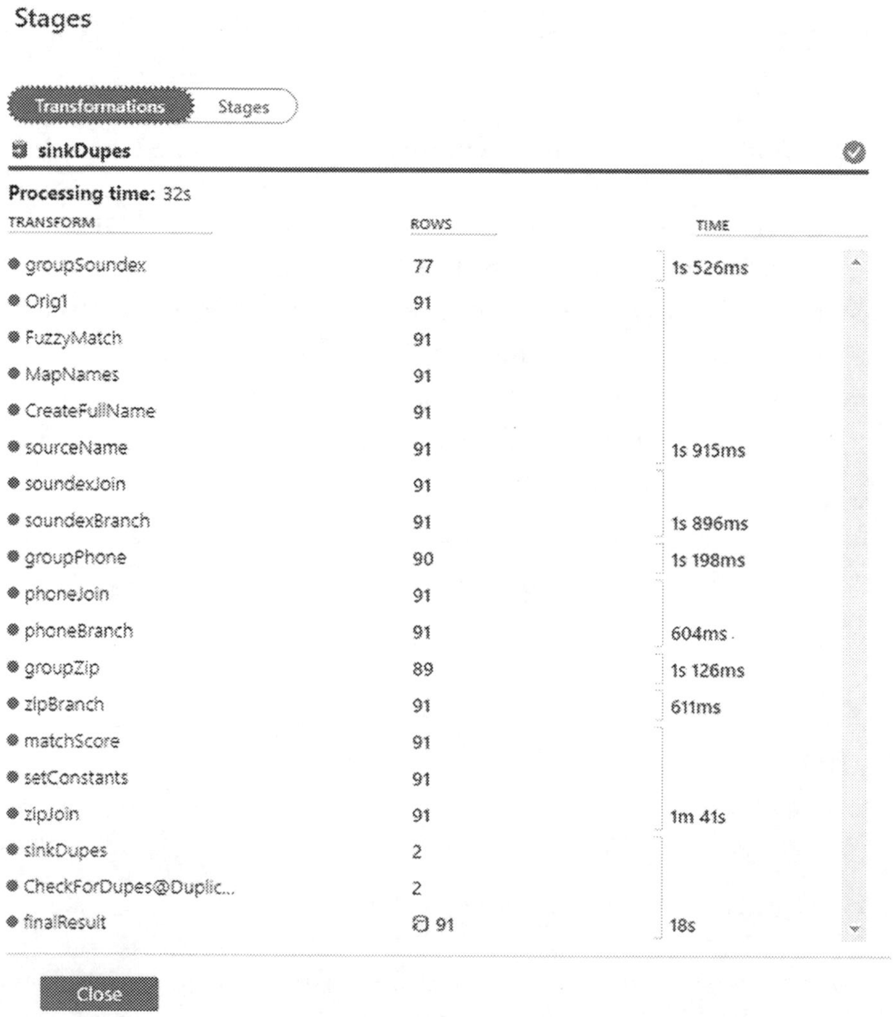

Stages

Transformations	Stages		
sinkDupes			✓

Processing time: 32s

TRANSFORM	ROWS	TIME
● groupSoundex	77	1s 526ms
● Orig1	91	
● FuzzyMatch	91	
● MapNames	91	
● CreateFullName	91	
● sourceName	91	1s 915ms
● soundexJoin	91	
● soundexBranch	91	1s 896ms
● groupPhone	90	1s 198ms
● phoneJoin	91	
● phoneBranch	91	604ms
● groupZip	89	1s 126ms
● zipBranch	91	611ms
● matchScore	91	
● setConstants	91	
● zipJoin	91	1m 41s
● sinkDupes	2	
● CheckForDupes@Duplic...	2	
● finalResult	⏱ 91	18s

Close

Figure 10-5. *Transformation stages*

Since we are looking closely at the sink transformation, let's also look at the "Merge file duration" property. In my version of this data flow, I set a blob sink to write to a single file in the sink properties. This is very common in ETL pipelines, but not a great practice in scale-out transformation patterns. I used this example to illustrate a point: ADF is built for scale. When you perform operations that are small-data oriented like writing many rows to a single file, there may be a penalty that is incurred. In this case, the overall performance of my pipeline suffered by one minute. Keep in mind that this is a demo scenario. In a real-world scenario with millions of rows, the cost of writing to a single file in the sink will be much greater. What happens in the Spark layer is that all of those partitions of distributed data that work so well for big data scenarios have to get coalesced back to a single partition in order to write a single file. Therefore, the best practice when writing files in ADF is to retain current partitioning of the sink when using file output.

The data flow execution plan graph includes the same search and zoom controls as the designer. When you zoom in, you will see a more detailed node icon for each transformation step. The boxes at the zoom level displayed in Figure 10-6 include indicators for each sink success or failure as well as a cache indicator to show when you had a successful cache hit with your data, meaning that ADF was able to perform transformations with additional source reads.

I would also like to point out an additional important data point that is visible on the top of Figure 10-6. Each data flow execution requires the Azure IR to have a Spark cluster available to run on. If you do not use the time-to-live (TTL) setting on the Azure IR for your data flows, then ADF will be required to spin up a new cluster for every data flow activity execution. The time it takes to acquire a live cluster can be in the range of three minutes. You'll see the total cluster acquisition time there.

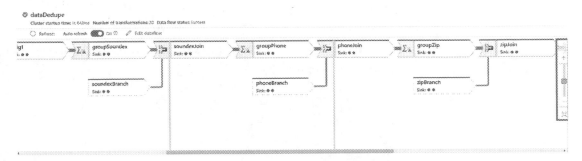

Figure 10-6. *Zoom in on the data flow execution graph*

Now that you have seen the basic parts of the Mapping Data Flow execution plan, let's talk a bit about how to use it to identify areas that could use performance optimizations. Start by looking at the pipeline view in Figure 10-1. Notice that the overall pipeline duration includes all activities in your pipeline. You can focus on the data flow activities in the pipeline and their durations when looking to optimize data flows. The total time that the pipeline registers for a data flow execution may differ from the cumulative time that is added up from each stage in your data flow monitoring view. That is because there is additional time that is accounted for in the pre- and postduration steps and the cluster acquisition time.

Next, sort the processing time column and look at the highest processing time. This will point you to the stages in your data flow that are taking the most time. Follow the aforementioned steps to locate your sinks and then open the sink details. Look for processing time that is outside of the total stage time. It is not uncommon to have blocking conditions on your destination databases or data lake when writing to cloud sources. But if your bottleneck is the transformation steps, then you may want to look at increasing the number of cores in your IR configuration or move to a memory-optimized IR.

Error Row Handling

When you are writing data to an Azure SQL sink, you can trap database errors returned by the database driver when your data is written from a pipeline execution. It is quite common to experience errors returned by the database that prevent rows from being committed to your target tables. In the following example, my database table has a NOT NULL constraint on the description column. If you do not enable error row handling, ADF is forced to terminate the job at that point, causing a pipeline failure. But if you enable error row handling in the database sink in your data flow, ADF can trap the errors and log the error rows for you, and you can even set the pipeline to return "success" rather than "failed" as a final status (see Figure 10-7).

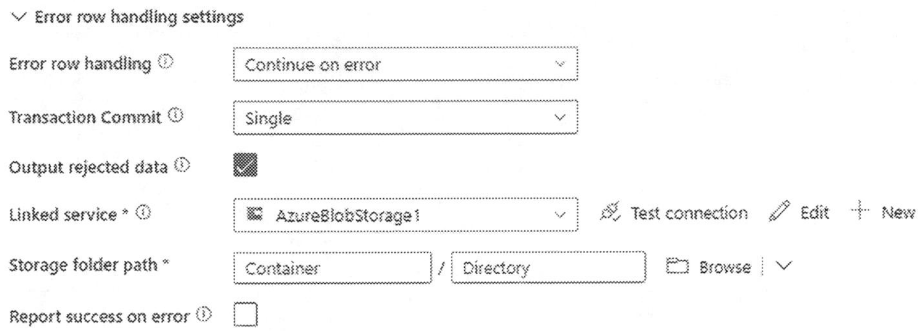

∨ Error row handling settings

Error row handling ⓘ   Continue on error ∨

Transaction Commit ⓘ   Single ∨

Output rejected data ⓘ   ▨

Linked service * ⓘ   🖼 AzureBlobStorage1 ∨   ⚡ Test connection ✎ Edit ＋ New

Storage folder path *   Container / Directory   🗀 Browse ∨

Report success on error ⓘ   ☐

Figure 10-7. *Set error row handling in Azure SQL Database sink*

ADF will write the error details to a CSV file in the location you specify and provide a couple of mechanisms to set control flow over the pipeline actions taken when these errors are encountered. First, choose "Continue on error", which means that when an error row is encountered, continue processing the data flow. The default setting in ADF is "Stop on first error", which means that the data flow will terminate when the first error is detected. If you choose to continue on error, you can then additionally choose to "Output rejected data" and "Report success on error". Reporting success on error is important because if you'd like your ETL job to process all rows and simply log, and then continue, theoretically you should set the activity return code to "success" in most of those cases. Otherwise, you will see a failure error code returned like in Figure 10-8.

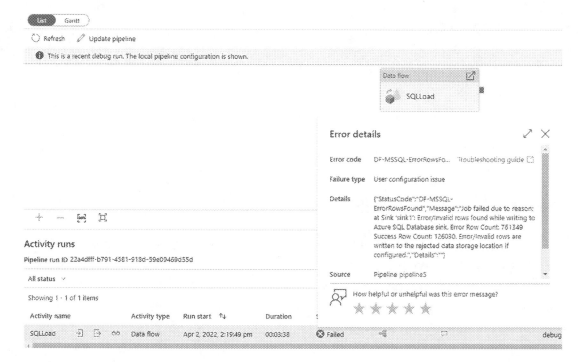

Figure 10-8. *Error code returned by data flow activity when "Stop on first error" is selected*

When outputting rejected rows to a text file, you will see an output file similar to the example in Figure 10-9. Every row that had an error is returned with the original values along with row-specific error returned by the database driver. As a next step, you can take this output and reprocess your ETL job using just the errored rows rather than having to have to reprocess the entire full source again.

BZ2 \"Message\":\"Cannot insert the value NULL into column [desc]

	BQ	BR	BS	BT	BU	BV	BW	BX	BY	BZ	CA
1	max_bal_	all_util	total_rev_	inq_fi	total_cu_t	inq_last_1	skid	DF_SQL_C	DF_Error_Details		
2			92500				715164	INSERT	[{\ErrorCo	\"Messag	table [dbo].[loansnew]; column does not allow nulls. INSERT fails.\"}]"
3			46400				715165	INSERT	[{\ErrorCo	\"Messag	table [dbo].[loansnew]; column does not allow nulls. INSERT fails.\"}]"
4			11500				715166	INSERT	[{\ErrorCo	\"Messag	table [dbo].[loansnew]; column does not allow nulls. INSERT fails.\"}]"
5			14300				715167	INSERT	[{\ErrorCo	\"Messag	table [dbo].[loansnew]; column does not allow nulls. INSERT fails.\"}]"
6			18200				245670	INSERT	[{\ErrorCo	\"Messag	table [dbo].[loansnew]; column does not allow nulls. INSERT fails.\"}]"
7			17300				715168	INSERT	[{\ErrorCo	\"Messag	table [dbo].[loansnew]; column does not allow nulls. INSERT fails.\"}]"
8			33200				245671	INSERT	[{\ErrorCo	\"Messag	table [dbo].[loansnew]; column does not allow nulls. INSERT fails.\"}]"
9			14800				715169	INSERT	[{\ErrorCo	\"Messag	table [dbo].[loansnew]; column does not allow nulls. INSERT fails.\"}]"
10			63200				245672	INSERT	[{\ErrorCo	\"Messag	table [dbo].[loansnew]; column does not allow nulls. INSERT fails.\"}]"
11	10919	35.4	161000	2	0	1	477055	INSERT	[{\ErrorCo	\"Messag	table [dbo].[loansnew]; column does not allow nulls. INSERT fails.\"}]"
12	2960	54	9000	0	0	-4	477056	INSERT	[{\ErrorCo	\"Messag	table [dbo].[loansnew]; column does not allow nulls. INSERT fails.\"}]"
13			8600				715170	INSERT	[{\ErrorCo	\"Messag	table [dbo].[loansnew]; column does not allow nulls. INSERT fails.\"}]"
14	4751	66.9	13300	2	0	0	477057	INSERT	[{\ErrorCo	\"Messag	table [dbo].[loansnew]; column does not allow nulls. INSERT fails.\"}]"
15			42700				715171	INSERT	[{\ErrorCo	\"Messag	table [dbo].[loansnew]; column does not allow nulls. INSERT fails.\"}]"
16	548	61	900	1	2	4	477058	INSERT	[{\ErrorCo	\"Messag	table [dbo].[loansnew]; column does not allow nulls. INSERT fails.\"}]"

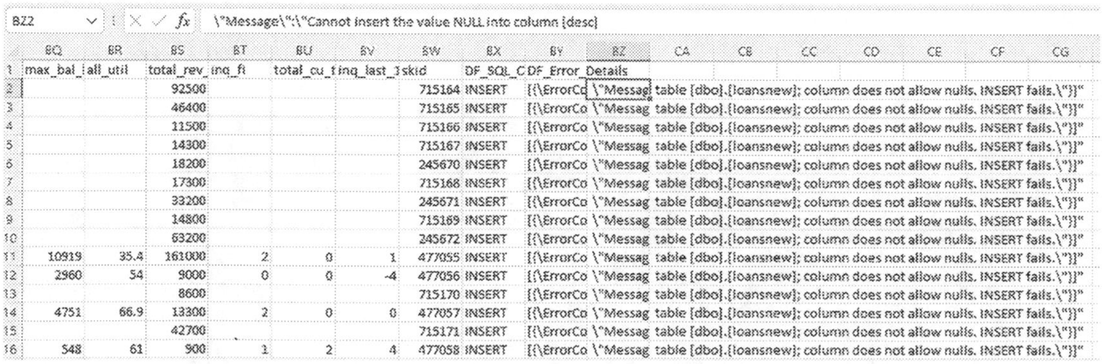

Figure 10-9. *Text output from error row handling*

The monitoring output from the activity monitoring view will show you all of the detailed telemetry from the execution of your Azure SQL Database sink when you have enabled error row handling (Figure 10-10). The following example shows the number of success rows, error rows, and the amount of time it took to write the error row log file. Notice that it took over one minute to write the log file. You should keep in mind that there will be a slight performance hit you will take when executing your data flows with error row handling enabled. There are additional steps needed to perform a two-phase commit operation that allows ADF to trap and report the error rows as well as use the Spark writer to output the log file for you.

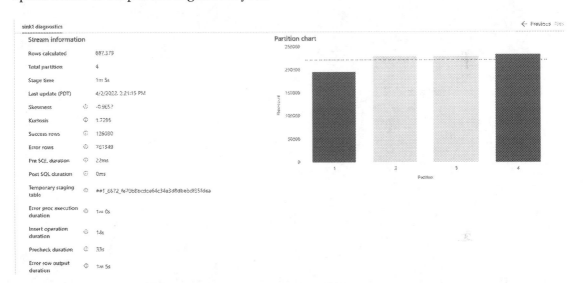

Figure 10-10. *Output in the monitoring view for data flows with error row handling enabled in Azure SQL Database sinks includes success rows, error rows, and the time it took to write the output data*

Partitioning Strategies

In the example shown earlier, take a quick look at the partitioning results from my pipeline execution in Figure 10-4. You can visually see from the diagram that my data is not well distributed across partitions. The skewness results in the monitoring view also give you indication that something is off. A value greater than (-/+)1 is outside of a normal distribution, meaning that you likely are experiencing data hotspots. This can occur occasionally when using default partitioning since Spark does not know anything about your data and so the data distribution can often appear skewed with no data in some partitions and other partitions completely empty. ADF provides a way for you to manually override the default partitioning and apply your own partition rules. In the Optimize tab on each transformation in the Mapping Data Flow design view, you can set your partitioning strategy (Figure 10-11). In the following example, I used source partitioning on my Azure SQL DB source. With database sources, source partitioning is a good practice to achieve best performance from database reads. You will then choose a high-cardinality column from your source database tables. I chose 8 partitions in this example because I matched the number of partitions with the number of cores (8) I had set for my worker nodes in the Azure IR.

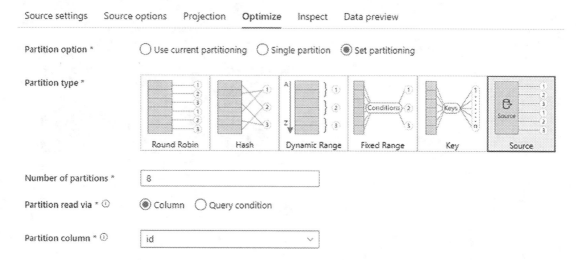

Figure 10-11. *Source partitioning set on the source transformation*

Round robin is another common partitioning you can consider using when you do not have an understanding of your data distribution but wish to limit or set the number of partitions. With round robin, ADF will create an even distribution of data across the partitions without regard to the data values. So if you were to ask for eight round robin partitions, you would see eight partitions in your data. However, if you have explored your data and are able to choose columns to create hash, the Hash Partitioning option can be very helpful and avoid data shuffling. You will supply the columns to hash, so it is important to only use hash distributions when you understand the data very well. This option helps to avoid data shuffling (a costly operation in Spark) because the common transformations you'll perform on your data can have all of the data in local partitions and avoid the penalty of redistributing data across worker nodes that you may incur in a round-robin or default partitioning strategy.

Optimizing Integration Runtimes

Data flow properties in the Azure Integration Runtime allow you to define the number of cores and the type of compute that ADF will use when managing Spark clusters for your data flows (Figure 10-12). Configuring your Azure IR for better performance by increasing the core count and compute type is an example of a "macro performance" tuning of your data flows because it will impact every pipeline that uses this Azure IR and does not affect your data flow logic.

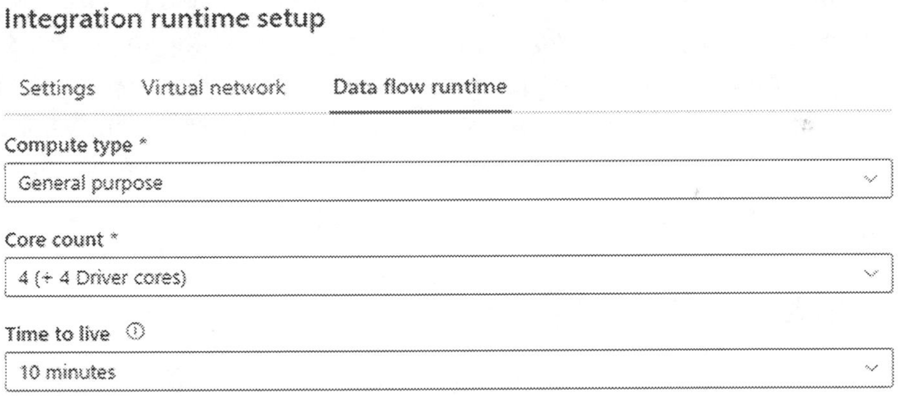

Integration runtime setup

| Settings | Virtual network | Data flow runtime |

Compute type *

General purpose   ∨

Core count *

4 (+ 4 Driver cores)   ∨

Time to live ⓘ

10 minutes   ∨

Figure 10-12. *Azure Integration Runtime setting for data flow runtime*

Compute Settings

When creating an Azure Integration Runtime (IR) for data flows, you will first need to consider the proper compute type and core count. You can create as many IRs in your factory as needed. There is no cost for having IR configurations stored in your factory. The only billing is incurred when they are used. It is a good practice to create IRs for small, medium, and large workloads that can be used for different purposes (i.e., dev, test, prod) and different workloads (i.e., initial load and incremental loads). The default IR settings are the lowest possible configurations: General Purpose (or basic) compute and eight cores (four driver cores, four worker cores). You should only need Memory Optimized (or standard) compute types when you have very long-running jobs that require large data frames where you read many files into memory, perform several joins and lookups, aggregate large datasets, or store many rows in cache.

The standard eight-core setting is good for debugging and testing sampled datasets. However, in most production workloads, you should use a minimum of 16 General Purpose (basic) cores. You can gain linear scale in many cases by adding more cores to your IR, but you must use current or default partitioning in your data flows to maximize that effect. If you set a static number of partitions, you will not always see a proportional performance boost as you add cores.

Alternatively, you can use the default AutoResolve IR for your data flow activities and set the compute type and core counts in the pipeline activity settings instead of creating new IRs. The benefit of this approach is that you can parameterize these properties so that each execution of your data flow is sized appropriately to the source data. The downside is that this creates a new configuration manifest for cluster provisioning on every iteration, meaning that you cannot use TTL when using the AutoResolve IR. Therefore, using the AutoResolve IR in the data flow pipeline activity will always incur the cold startup time latency.

Time to Live (TTL)

ADF manages the Spark environment for you and can maintain that cluster for your factory based on the time-to-live setting. This is useful when you execute many short-lived ETL jobs in ADF. The cold start-up time for a normal data flow activity when there is not an active warm pool available is approximately three minutes. For long-running ETL jobs that take one hour to complete, a three-minute delay is not significant in terms of overall SLA or costs. However, if you are executing 60 one-minute jobs in an hour, you would have to incur that startup 60 times, making the overall pipeline time over 3x longer and breaking your SLA.

A good solution to this is to set a small (ten minutes) TTL that will instruct ADF to maintain a cluster for each of your Azure IRs that you use. The TTL and the cluster maintained are based on the integration runtime, and you can benefit from the TTL with sequential data flow activity execution even in different pipelines. If the next data flow activity is issued within that TTL time, each job will start up in just a few seconds. A small TTL is usually sufficient. Setting a very long TTL (i.e., two hours or four hours) is very rare and should only be used in unusual circumstances where you are certain that you wish to have ADF maintain a cluster for long periods of time in a warm state. The default for new IRs is ten minutes, which is typically a good starting point for most workloads.

Iterating over Files

The pattern I spoke of earlier with many data flows executed in sequence vs. in parallel is a very common architectural decision to be made by ADF data engineers. In ADF's pipeline workflows, you can put a data flow activity inside of a For Each loop to iterate over a list of files. Inside of the For Each, you can control the parallelism with a batch count property and a switch for setting the execution pattern to sequential. The best practice for data flows is to use sequential iteration in For Each with a ten-minute TTL in the IR to take full advantage of the cluster reuse feature in ADF. If that pattern does not fit into your SLA, then consider a small batch count in parallel mode in the For Each with a ten-minute TTL. For example, if you are iterating over 100 files and set a batch count of 10, ADF will form 10 clusters for you based on the configuration set in your Azure IR. On the next batch, ADF will be able to reuse the existing warm clusters, so you'll only incur the cold startup time on the first batch. If you are going to use this pattern, it is best to consider a small size of cores and compute type since you will hydrate a large number of clusters.

An alternative to this pattern is to avoid the For Each in the pipeline and instead use the source transformation inside of the data flow itself to bring a set of files or folders into the data frame. To do this, you would use the wildcard or list of files option in the source transformation. This pattern will operate much more efficiently than through execution of individual data flow jobs via a For Each iterator. However, it is not always feasible. ADF will try to create data frames that include the full schema from every file that is being read. If your schemas vary, or if you have more files than can be fit into memory in worker nodes, you will have to use the For Each approach instead.

Parameterizing

Parameterizing your data flows is a great way to create generalized data flows that can be reused without creating many of the same patterns over and over. Earlier in the book, I introduced the concept of Flowlets for logical component reuse in Mapping Data Flows. Flowlets are an important aspect of componentizing your transformations and maximizing reuse to optimize the size of your data factories. In other words, avoid creating data factory artifact sprawl with a lot of individual data flows that are purpose built for just one pattern. Additionally, parameterization in ADF is a concept that flows throughout the ADF ecosystem and allows you to pass parameters from pipelines to your data flows and even into datasets and linked service connections. From an optimization perspective, what this capability does is to allow you to write fewer data flow graphs and maintain a smaller, easier-to-manage factory size. However, to achieve this, you will need to implement the concepts we talked about earlier in the book that are called "late column binding."

Pipeline Parameters

Parameterizing pipelines is very important in ADF to avoid generating many pipelines for similar scenarios, thereby creating a cluttered factory. Instead, it is preferable to create generic patterns (just like we've been talking about in this book with regard to data flow patterns) with pipelines that can be configured via parameters. Both pipeline parameters (Figure 10-13) and data flow parameters can be accessed by clicking on the diagram designer on any open white space. Under "Parameters" in the bottom panel, you will be able to manage your parameters.

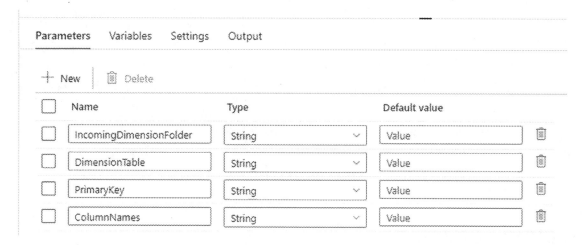

Figure 10-13. *Pipeline parameters*

For this book, we are focused on Mapping Data Flows, so I'm not going to go into detail of the pipeline expression builder like we have for data flows (Figure 10-14). You will notice, however, that the expression language is different in pipeline expressions than in data flow expressions. The primary reason for this is that the pipeline engine uses Logic Apps for workflow orchestrations, whereas data flow is a data transformation scale-out engine built on Apache Spark. There is a different intent that needs to be expressed for workflows than for data transformations, so one grammar does not suffice for both workloads.

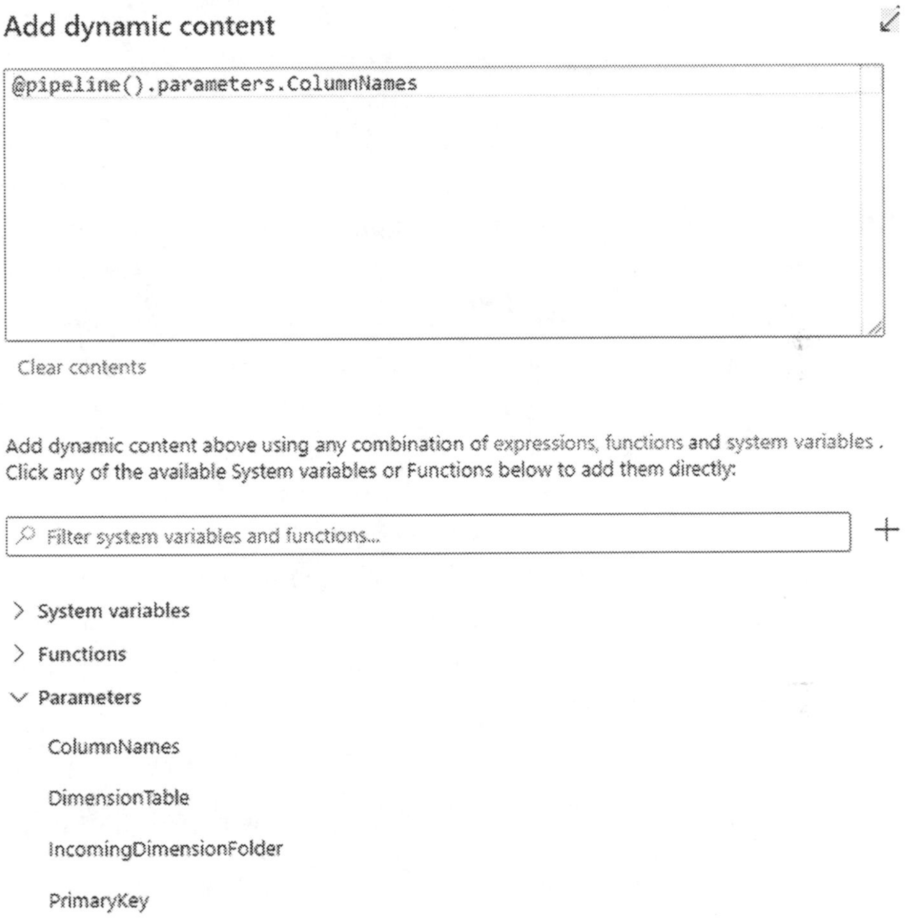

Add dynamic content

```
@pipeline().parameters.ColumnNames
```

Clear contents

Add dynamic content above using any combination of expressions, functions and system variables .
Click any of the available System variables or Functions below to add them directly:

🔍 Filter system variables and functions...   +

> System variables

> Functions

∨ Parameters

ColumnNames

DimensionTable

IncomingDimensionFolder

PrimaryKey

Figure 10-14. *The pipeline expression builder UI*

For now, let's stay within the context of data flow activities in your pipeline. When you add a data flow activity that has parameters, you will see the argument list under "Parameters" in the bottom panel of the pipeline designer (Figure 10-15).

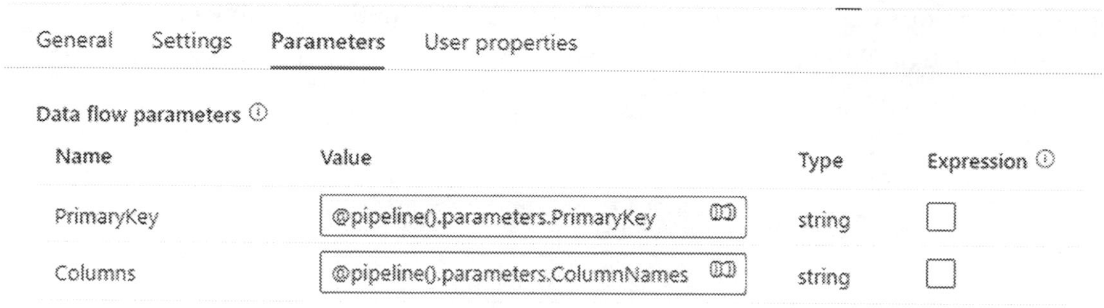

General	Settings	**Parameters**	User properties

Data flow parameters ⓘ

Name	Value	Type	Expression ⓘ
PrimaryKey	@pipeline().parameters.PrimaryKey ⫘	string	☐
Columns	@pipeline().parameters.ColumnNames ⫘	string	☐

Figure 10-15. *Setting data flow parameters from the pipeline activity*

When you click inside the Value box, you will see an option to enter your parameter value either using a data flow expression or a pipeline expression (Figure 10-16). You can use whichever language you are more comfortable with here. Keep in mind a few caveats: only the pipeline expression will be able to access parameters and variables that you have set in the pipeline context. The example shown in Figure 10-15 is referencing pipeline parameters. You will need to use the pipeline expression to enter a value like you see there: `@pipeline().parameters.PrimaryKey`. If you choose data flow expression, you will see a data flow expression builder launch inside of your pipeline editor where you can build expressions using the Mapping Data Flow data transformation expression language.

Figure 10-16. *You have an option of setting parameter values from the pipeline using data flow expressions or pipeline expressions*

Another very common type of parameterization in ADF is parameterization of Datasets and Linked Services. Pipelines and data flows fully support parameters in both of the objects. To set parameters in datasets and linked services, you will set the values in the Settings tab on the data flow activity (Figure 10-17).

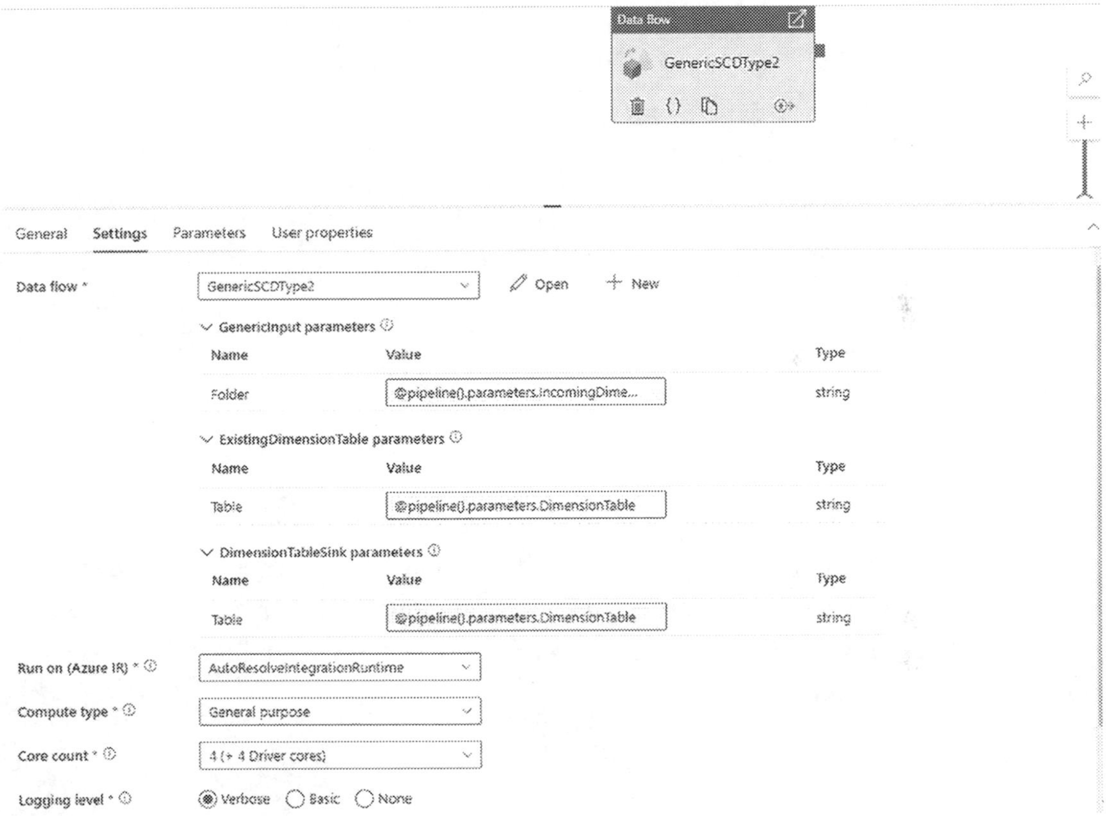

Figure 10-17. *Parameterization of datasets used inside of a data flow*

Data Flow Parameters

To create parameters inside your data flows that can receive values from a pipeline, click on the Mapping Data Flow designer surface whitespace and select "Parameters" on the bottom panel (Figure 10-18). Here, you can create parameters and set default values for each parameter.

Figure 10-18. *Parameters panel in Mapping Data Flows*

Once you have your parameters defined, you can use the parameter values throughout your data flow logic (see Figure 10-19). Inside of the expression builder, you will see a Parameters section under "Expression elements". When you select Parameters, you will see the parameters that you already created. You can also create new parameters from the expression builder.

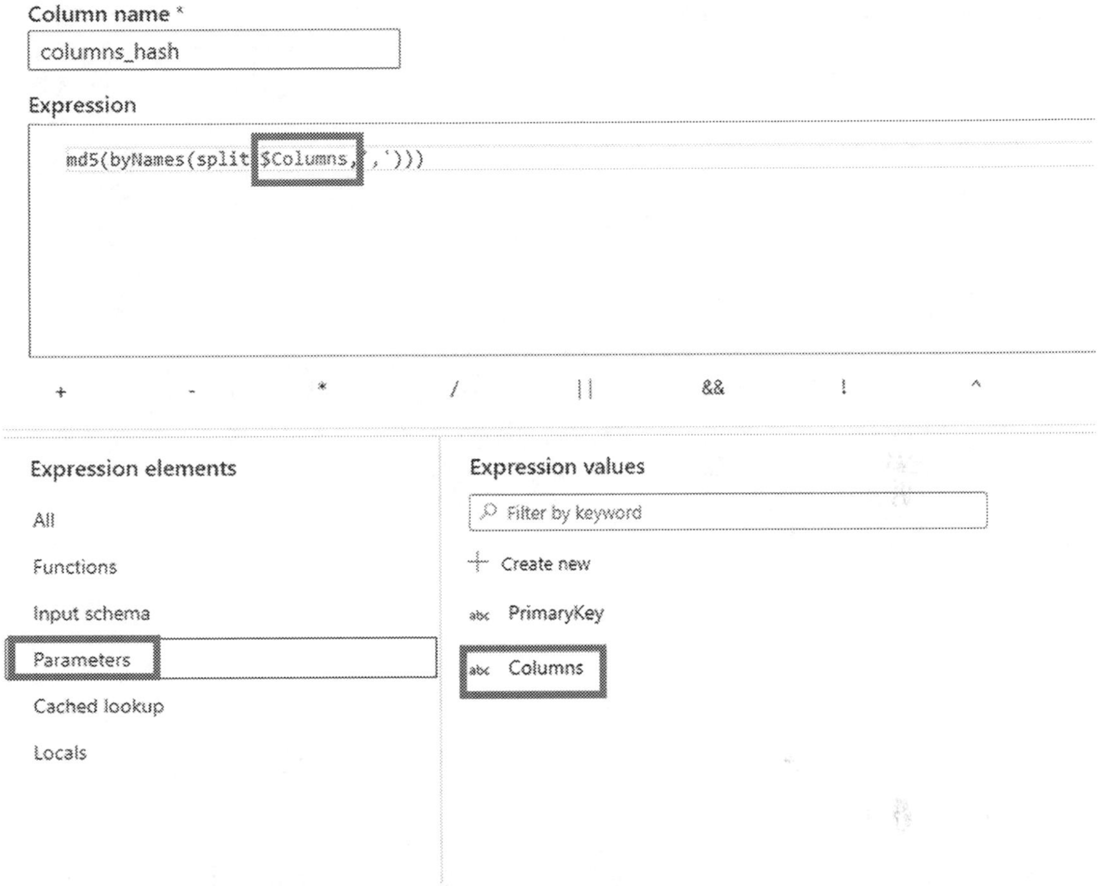

Column name *

columns_hash

Expression

```
md5(byNames(split($Columns, ,`)))
```

| + | - | * | / | \|\| | && | ! | ^ |

Expression elements

All

Functions

Input schema

Parameters

Cached lookup

Locals

Expression values

🔍 Filter by keyword

＋ Create new

abc PrimaryKey

abc Columns

Figure 10-19. Using parameters inside of your data flow

Once your parameters have been added to the data flow, you can access the values using the $param syntax. The example in Figure 10-19 shows $Columns as parameter in the expression.

When debugging data flows with parameters, you must either have a default value already set for each parameter or you can set and override each value from the Parameters in Debug settings (Figure 10-20). You must have a value for each parameter before you can use data preview to view your transformation results while debugging.

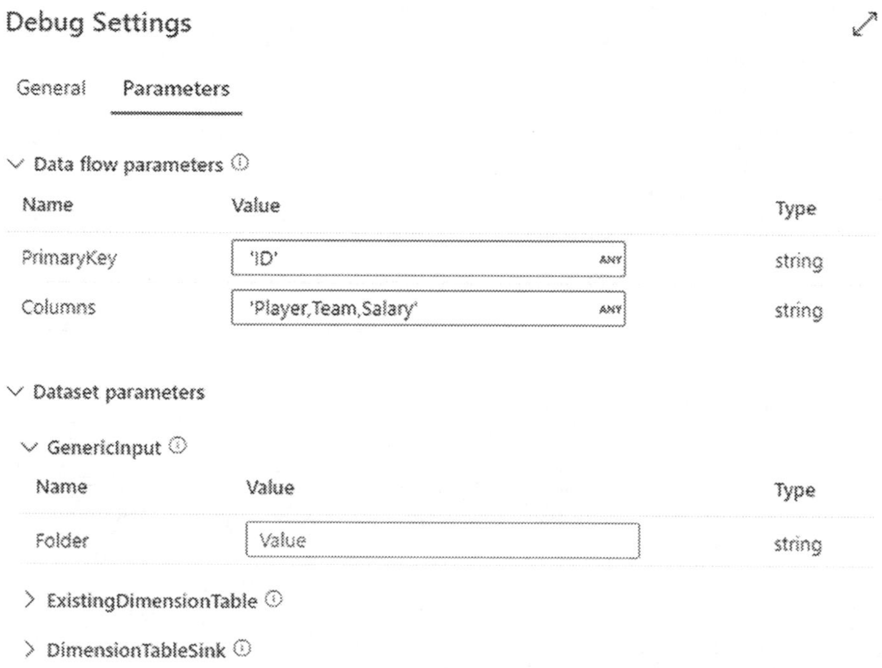

Debug Settings   ↗

General   **Parameters**

∨ Data flow parameters ⓘ

Name	Value		Type
PrimaryKey	'ID' ANY	string
Columns	'Player,Team,Salary' ANY	string

∨ Dataset parameters

∨ GenericInput ⓘ

Name	Value		Type
Folder	Value		string

> ExistingDimensionTable ⓘ

> DimensionTableSink ⓘ

Figure 10-20. *Setting data flow parameters for data preview and debugging*

Late Binding

In order to fully take advantage of this reuse and generalization pattern in ADF Mapping Data Flows, you will want to write transformations that utilize "late column binding" whereby the names of the fields you are transforming are not known until runtime. This makes the design-time environment a little more tricky because you will not have a full set of metadata available to you such that column inspection will not be visible and auto-complete will not include metadata. But it will make your patterns much more reusable, resulting in fewer data flows in your factory resources. To use this technique in Mapping Data Flows, make sure to use column patterns in transformations, byName() to find column names in your data, enable schema drift in your sources and sinks, and use auto-mapping in your sink. We talked earlier in the book about creating a semantic model inside of your data flow using a Derived Column transformation. This can be helpful in late binding scenarios such that you can then refer to column names generated in the derived column later downstream in your data flow.

Data Profiling

When you are looking to optimize your data transformation logic, a good place to start is by gaining meaningful insights into your data through data exploration. When you understand your data patterns and topology, you can set the appropriate optimizations. To that end, ADF provides data profiling capabilities in Mapping Data Flows, which allows data engineers to view statistics about your data that includes value distributions, number of nulls, duplicate values, and ranges.

Mapping Data Flow Statistics

Inside of the data preview panel on each transformation in ADF, there are many ways to explore your data and discover deep insights about the shape and profile of the data that you are working with.

Data Preview Statistics

The most common and easiest way to see a data profile is from the data preview pane (Figure 10-21). Select a column in your data preview and then click on "Statistics". ADF will profile your data based on the sampling size listed in the debug settings. If you'd like to profile your entire dataset, set a large number in the source "Row limit" property under debug settings.

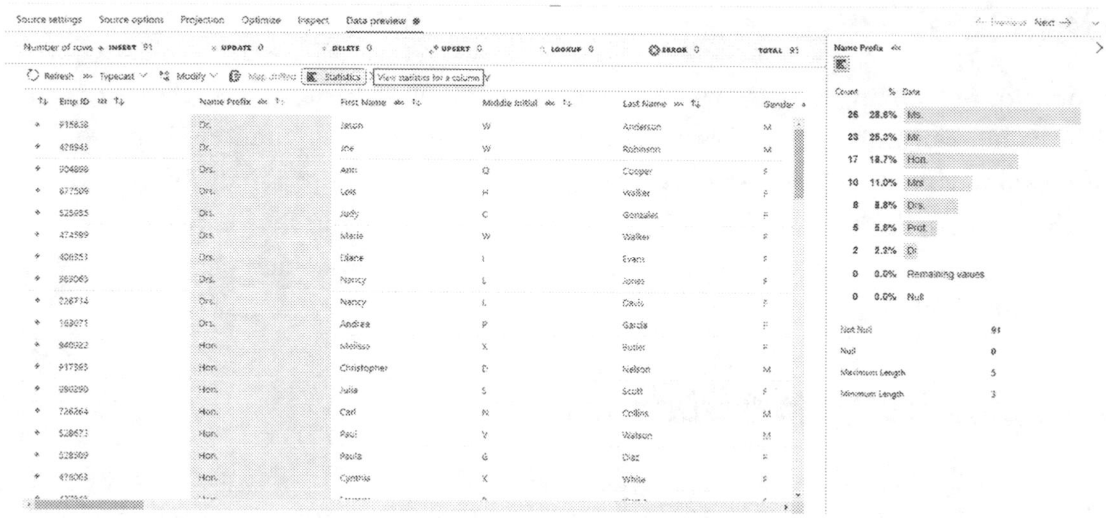

Figure 10-21. *Data preview with column profile statistics*

Profile Stats

Earlier in the book, I introduced you to the data flow script behind the visual graphs in ADF's Mapping Data Flows. You can take snippets of that script and share it in other data flows. The following is an example of a script snippet taken from a data flow that uses many of the advanced features we've been discussing: '$$' as 'this' operator and column patterns. This snippet is completely generic and can be used in any data flow. It will check the data types of each incoming column in your dataset and provide the results of profiling your data. Add an Aggregate transformation to your data flow, call it "SummaryStats", and then open the code behind using the script button. Paste this snippet in place of the current SummaryStats script definition:

```
aggregate(each(match(true()), $$+'_NotNull' = countIf(!isNull($$)), $$ +
'_Null' = countIf(isNull($$))),
        each(match(type=='double'||type=='integer'||type=='short'||type==
        'decimal'), $$+'_stddev' = round(stddev($$),2), $$ + '_min' = min
        ($$), $$ + '_max' = max($$), $$ + '_average' = round(avg($$),2),
        $$ + '_variance' = round(variance($$),2)),
        each(match(type=='string'), $$+'_maxLength' = max(length($$)))) ~>
        SummaryStats
```

The output you will see will include the number of null values, standard deviation, min, max, average, variance, and max length. Use the "export csv" button on the data preview pane to export the preview results with your summary statistics and keep a copy to refer back to. You use it to determine which columns are good candidates for hashing based on value distributions. You leverage the information about null values to add logic in your data flow to handle nulls using replacement values as a way to handle data cleaning.

Power Query Activity

Another interesting way to explore and inspect your data is to use the Power Query activity from the ADF pipeline. To do this, create a new Power Query from factory resources (Figure 10-22).

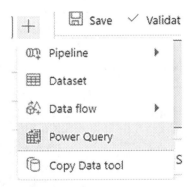

Figure 10-22. *Create a new Power Query*

Now all you have to do is to add a dataset that you wish to explore (Figure 10-23). You will not transform data or even need a pipeline for data profiling with Power Query. In this use case, we are simply using Power Query as a way to better understand our data patterns, not to execute from a pipeline.

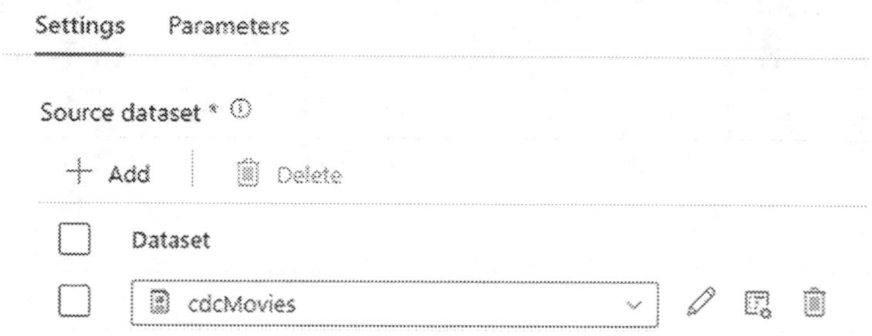

Figure 10-23. *Choose a dataset for your Power Query*

Inside of the Power Query UI, go to Options ➤ Global options (Figure 10-24). Turn on the column profile options and set the profile evaluation to the top 1,000 rows. You can use the entire dataset option, but be aware that when you are working with Power Query interactively in this scenario, you are not accessing the ADF scale-out compute in the IR. For that reason, exploring large datasets in Power Query interactively has limited compute resources available to it.

If you build a set of transformations from Power Query and then execute it from a pipeline, you will then benefit from the Mapping Data Flow scale-out Spark compute environment. For simple data exploration across a large dataset when using Power Query, utilize the profile evaluation sampling.

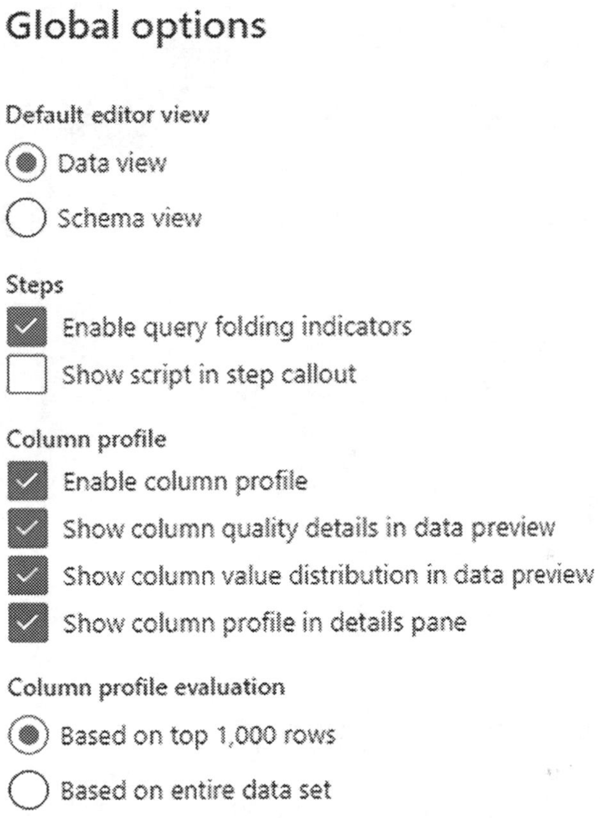

Global options

Default editor view

◉ Data view

◯ Schema view

Steps

☑ Enable query folding indicators

☐ Show script in step callout

Column profile

☑ Enable column profile

☑ Show column quality details in data preview

☑ Show column value distribution in data preview

☑ Show column profile in details pane

Column profile evaluation

◉ Based on top 1,000 rows

◯ Based on entire data set

Figure 10-24. *Turn on column profiles in the Power Query activity*

Once you've set those options, you will now see a full set of column profile statistics at the top of the data grid (Figure 10-25). The advantage of this approach over the ADF data preview pane is that here you will see the results for all columns as opposed to the Mapping Data Flow UI where you must first select each column individually and then manually click the statistics button.

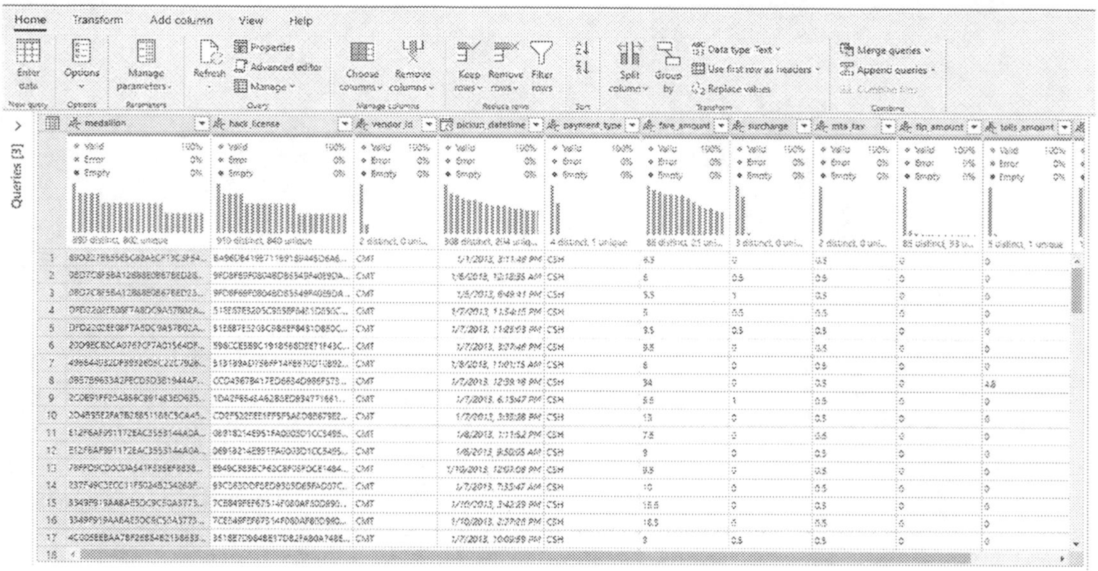

Figure 10-25. *Column profiles in Power Query*

Transformation Optimization

Let's take a brief look at a couple of very common optimizations that you can apply at the transformation level in your data flows by improving your data flow logic on a micro level.

byName( ) and byNames( )

These metafunctions are the most common way to find metadata in your dataset when the schema is unknown or evolving. Metafunctions like byName() are very important in supporting the ADF concept of late column binding and building reusable data flow patterns that are generic. An example of using byNames() is shown in the following. In this example, we're using byNames() as a way to find every column that matches an array of string column names in the $Column parameter:

```
md5(byNames(split($Columns,',')))
```

What we're doing with that statement is asking ADF to find every occurrence of a list of columns in the data and apply an md5 hash to each row value of each column.

Rank and Surrogate Key

Inside of the Window transformation are three very common aggregate functions that only work within the Window transformation: rank(), denseRank(), and rowNumber(). These operations are so common in ETL pipelines that ADF created transformations just for the use cases that leverage those functions. The advantage of using the purpose-built transformations is that they have built-in logic to optimize performance for ranking and unique row numbers, whereas the Window transformation is a general-purpose transformation for analytical and aggregate functions across partitioned data windows. For the use case of assigning a unique number to each row, it is best practice to use the Surrogate Key transformation and for the case of ranking data use the Rank transformation (Figure 10-26).

Figure 10-26. *The surrogate key and rank transformation*

Sorting

Sorting is an expensive operation because ADF is required to first sort across multiple partitions. The impact of that operation is that you'll need to set the "single partition" option in the Optimize tab on the sort transformation in order to bring all of the data into a single partition for sorting order. If you don't do this, you'll end up with data that is out of order because the partition ordering is nondeterministic.

Database Queries

In the source transformation, you can improve the overall performance of data flows that have database sources by pushing down the source query as well as aggregations and other functions in your source query (Figure 10-27). You can also gain additional performance boosts by leveraging source database stored procedures. Another way to adjust the performance of your database reads is to set a large batch size when using a memory-optimized Azure IR with a high number of cores. The isolation level can also be set here and can have an impact on the performance of your database reads. You can set it to be very permissive and read uncommitted data, where you accept the possibility of dirty reads. At the other extreme, you can use "serializable" to ensure that only committed transactions are read while incurring the performance penalty of read locks.

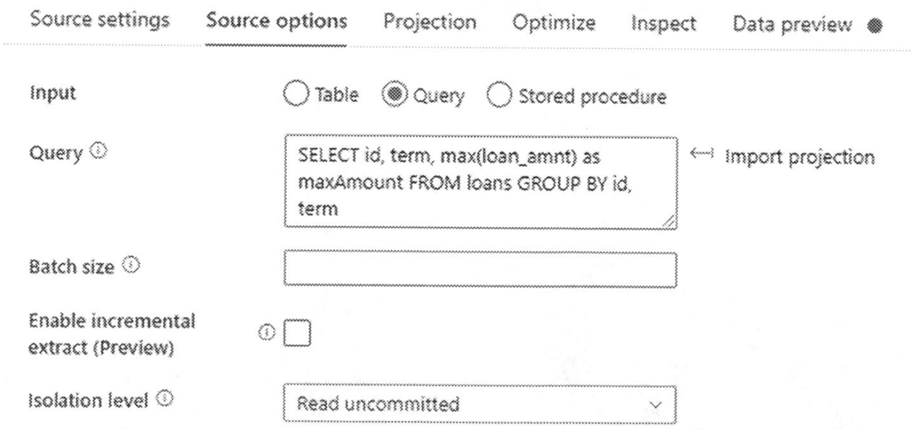

Figure 10-27. *Source data queries are pushed down into the source database*

Joins and Lookups

Joins and lookups are very common operations in ETL jobs, and in ADF's Mapping Data Flows, there are several important optimizations that you utilize. You may also find that using a memory-optimized Integration Runtime may also improve the performance of your joins and lookups.

Broadcasting

In the Join and Lookup transformations, you'll find an option called "Broadcast" under the Optimize tab (see Figure 10-28). Broadcasting is a mechanism that ADF can use in Spark when executing your data flow. Spark is a distributed computing environment, so joins (ADF Lookup is also a join) can be tricky when the data is split up. Spark stores data in memory using DataFrames, and when combined with data distribution, Spark becomes very effective when processing large datasets. However, when you perform operations like joins and not all of the data you are joining happens to be local to the worker node, data shuffling will occur, which can have a negative impact on your data flow performance. If you set the broadcast option on, you are telling ADF to use the Spark broadcast features that will send the DataFrames from either the left, the right, or both sides of the join operation to the Spark worker node executors. When you have a lot of join operations in your data flow, you may find that you benefit from higher core counts and memory-optimized IRs. By forcing very large datasets into worker nodes using broadcast, your data flow has the potential to fail with "out-of-memory" errors. It is best to keep this setting to "Auto" and let ADF make the best choice for you. In general, broadcasting the smaller side of the relationship is a good practice. There are also conditions in Joins in ADF that will require you to turn on broadcasting such as non-equijoins.

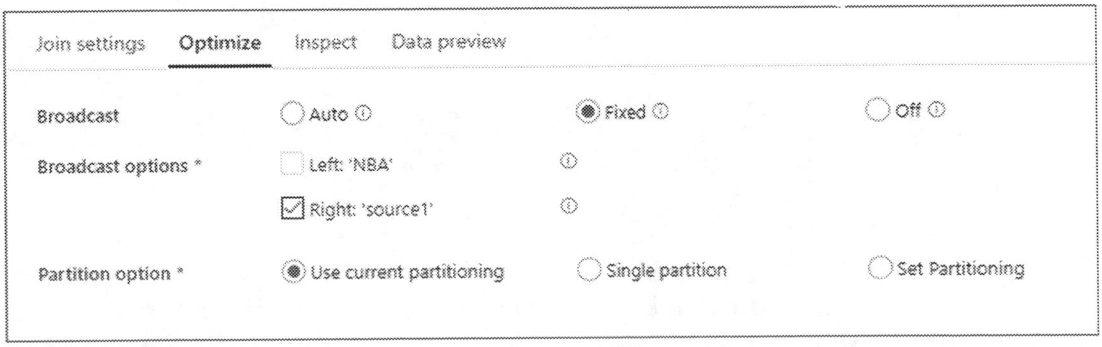

Figure 10-28. Broadcast join

Cached Lookup

The Lookup transformation in ADF reads data from the relationships defined in the transformation configuration for every row. When performing lookups in your logic, you will likely find that the cached lookup mechanism can perform better. A disadvantage to using cached lookups is that you will be limited to how much data you can store in the cache by the amount of RAM available in the worker nodes on your cluster. Use the feature conservatively as it will consume memory resources on your Azure IR.

To use cached lookups, first generate your cached sink by using a sink of type "cache" (Figure 10-29).

Figure 10-29. *Cached sink*

Once you've added a cached sink to your data flow, you will now be able to store data in that sink for reference later using the lookup(), output(), and outputs() functions. In the example in Figure 10-29, I've stored a row count aggregation in the sink called "cachedSink". I did not set any key columns (found on the sink settings tab), and I only mapped the "rowcount" column. To access that stored cached value from my data flow, I created DerivedColumn1. From there, I can access that stored aggregated value using this expression (Figure 10-30): `cachedSink#outputs().rowcount`. If I had stored a key column in my cached sink, I would then need to supply a lookup value for the cached lookup this way: `cachedSink#lookup(key1)`.

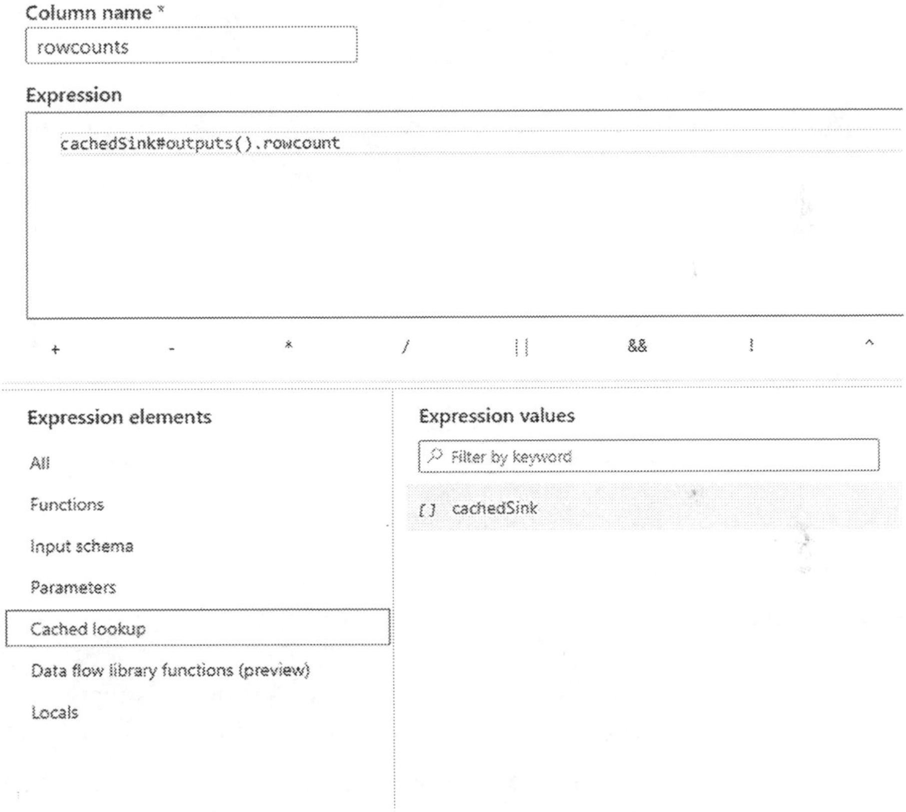

Figure 10-30. *Cached lookup and cached sink inside the expression builder*

Pipeline Optimizations for Data Flow Activity

There are several settings in the data flow pipeline activity that can have an effect on your data flow and pipeline performance (see Figure 10-31).

General   **Settings**   Parameters   User properties

Data flow *   SQLLoad   ⌄   ✎ Open   + New

Run on (Azure IR) * ⓘ   AutoResolveIntegrationRuntime   ⌄

Compute type * ⓘ   General purpose   ⌄

Core count * ⓘ   4 (+ 4 Driver cores)   ⌄

Logging level * ⓘ   ◉ Verbose   ◯ Basic   ◯ None

> ⌄ Sink properties
>
> Run in parallel ⓘ   ☐
>
> Continue after sink error ⓘ ☐
>
> ⌄ Staging ⓘ
>
> Staging linked service ⓘ   Select...   ⌄   + New
>
> Staging storage folder   Container   /   Directory   🗁 Browse ⌄

Figure 10-31. *Data flow activity pipeline settings*

Run in Parallel

When you have a data flow that has sinks in the same group inside of a stream (as shown in Figure 10-32), you can set the "Run in parallel" option in the data flow activity setting in the pipeline. When you have a sink that is taking time to coalesce files or has a long-running database write operation, you can gain an overall data flow performance boost by setting run in parallel to on so that ADF can write to the other sinks while the other sinks are busy.

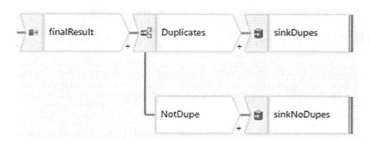

Figure 10-32. *Data flow sinks in the same stream group*

Logging Level

From the pipeline, you can set the logging level for your data flow execution. The options are verbose, basic, and none. When you are testing your pipelines or are troubleshooting a production data flow, it is a good practice to turn on verbose logging. Verbose will provide all of the statistical and partition details for each execution. However, there is a small overhead that can have a slight impact on performance. Therefore, you can set the logging level to basic to relieve some of the telemetry collection, possibly gaining a bit of performance at the expense of full-fidelity logging. Lastly, you can choose to not log the execution details at all and forgo all of the execution plan details that we spoke of in this chapter. This option is usually not a great trade-off for the performance boost you may see. A good use case for no logging would be when you have a very simple data flow that you do not require to have execution plans stored.

Database Staging

Any database that you connect to from ADF that utilizes a staging pattern for reading or writing data will benefit from setting the "enable staging" checkbox option. For example, when reading or writing with Azure Synapse Analytics databases, it is always recommended to use staging in ADF. In large data warehouse scenarios, the data stores are often able to leverage built-in fast loader utilities that can bulk load and bulk read using staging.

Summary

In this chapter, we monitored our triggered pipelines and debug runs from the ADF monitoring UI. After looking for pipeline success and failure, we saw the execution time for each pipeline and every transformation in our data flows. I showed you how to read the detailed data flow activity execution plans and then how to put that together into a variety of optimization strategies. We talked about using a tiered approach to performance reviews and optimizations by considering optimizing at a macro level through integration runtime settings and micro-level performance tuning through data and logic introspection.

Index

A

Address dataset, 55
addressIdUnique, 60
adf_publish, 148
ADLS Gen2 dataset, 64
Aggregate, 41
Aggregate transformation, 135
Alter Row transformation, 43
Arrays, 127, 128
Assert, 43
Assert transformation, 54, 58, 59
AutoResolve IR, 166
Avro format, 133
AzureBlobStorage1, 19
Azure data factory (ADF), 12, 13, 27, 53
    artifacts, 15, 144
    collaboration branch, 144
    concepts, 13, 14
    data flows, 131
    data flow expression language, 128
    data preview pane, 179
    expression language, 44
    Git to the DataOps world, 145
    interpretation, 157
    live mode, 150
    and Mapping Data Flows, 32, 79, 92, 124, 126, 155
    monitoring view, 156
    overview, 13
    parameterization, 167, 171
    pipelines, 15, 18
    Publish branch, 144
    resources, 14
    schedule trigger, 151
    service, 146
    storage events triggers, 15, 152
    trigger now option, 151
    tumbling window trigger, 151
    pipeline, 50
Azure DevOps (ADO), 142, 143, 146
Azure Functions, 15
Azure integration runtime, 16, 17, 46, 47, 165
Azure portal, 140, 141
Azure SQL Database, 6, 73, 161

B

Blob storage account, 19
Body.properties.periods, 121
Bookbranch, 145
Boolean expression, 39
Branch, 145, 150
Broadcasting, 183, 184
Business intelligence tools, 6

C

Cached lookup, 45
Cached sink, 184
CacheKey, 84
CI/CD processes, 139
Cloud-based ETL
    in Azure, 5
    serving layer, 6

Printed in the United States
by Baker & Taylor Publisher Services